Finding Happiness When It Hurts

A little book of comfort for when being happy feels out of reach

LISA BRETT

Finding Happiness When It Hurts

ISBN 978-1-907308-03-1

First published in the UK by Compass-Publishing UK, 2022.
Typeset and Edited by The Book Refinery Ltd.
www.TheBookRefinery.com

www.LisaBrettAuthor.com

Printed and bound by CMP, Dorset, UK.
This book has been produced using Carbon Capture paper, creating native woodland in the UK.

This book is dedicated to my beloved golden Labrador,
Daisy Boo.

My best friend, and my constant and faithful companion.
Love of my life. My saviour.

Ti voglio bene.
(I love you.)

Foreword

by Rachel Kelly

There's not much to recommend depression. However, one of the best things that happened to me after I wrote a memoir in 2014 about my own mental health struggles was that others who'd found life hard got in touch. They too had struggled, they too had visited very dark places, and they too had found ways through.

So it was that my path crossed with Lisa Brett's, someone who also knew what it was to feel traumatised. Indeed, Lisa, like me, got to the stage when she didn't want to live anymore.

Thank goodness she did live, because she has gone on to recover, thanks to what she describes as a 'spiritual awakening', when the Universe intervened on her behalf. And the result is her comforting and uplifting book *Finding Happiness When It Hurts*.

Lisa says she found writing about both the blackness she'd experienced and how she managed to find blessings in adversity was cathartic. Her writing has also provided a valuable gift for us readers.

Not only does Lisa share 'Blessing bites' – nuggets of wisdom that got me thinking in a different way – she also shares the stories of others: Amanda Lynch, for example, who writes movingly about how her curly-haired, black poodle helped her with her breast cancer diagnosis and chemotherapy; or the story of Cilla Peck, who writes about how an accident gave her time to look after her new granddaughter.

Blessings come in unexpected places – places revealed and unearthed by Lisa in ways that mean we too can maybe find benefits in what might otherwise seem very dark moments.

These voices give the book a richness, thanks to the diversity of experiences they record. So too does another voice in the book – that of a character called Gaia; this is the name for Mother Earth and also someone Lisa describes as her higher or intuitive self. Gaia strikes up conversations with those she meets on a beach, which is a place where Lisa herself most readily finds the rainbows that come with the storms.

I've sometimes struggled to listen to my own higher self. From reading Gaia's exchanges, I believe that Lisa's right when she says she feels her book came through her from some spirit from beyond. I know I sometimes feel that about my own writing, when it seems to come easily and effortlessly: it comes through me; I am just a vehicle for something more universal.

Throughout the book, you'll find images of butterflies. As Lisa says, these creatures teach us much; they're important in the spiritual world as symbols of transformation.

As Lisa also states, for many of us, becoming ourselves and finding our own inner wisdom and truth requires change, just as a butterfly undergoes a transformation when it breaks out of its chrysalis. Lisa herself has undergone great change. In this heartfelt and moving book, she generously shares what she has learned. I, for one, finished reading it having been helped. My own learning never stops, and Lisa has helped me on my continuing journey.

Rachel Kelly is a mental health advocate and Sunday Times bestselling author of Black Rainbow: How words healed me – my journey through depression. *Her book* You'll Never Walk Alone: Poems for life's ups and downs *will be published in November 2022.*[1]

---

1. Kelly, R (2022). *You'll Never Walk Alone: Poems for life's ups and downs*. London: Hodder & Stoughton. Available from: https://uk.bookshop.org/books/you-ll-never-walk-alone-poems-for-life-s-ups-and-downs/9781529395341

Contents

Blessings – 21

Finding the Blessings

Finding Happiness When It Hurts will remind you to feel and show gratitude when things go right, but also show you how to find the blessings when things go wrong.

The simple reason for this being that if you change the way you think about things when you're having a hard time, it can make you feel better. Making a conscious decision to shift gear from negative to positive gives a different perspective, and it's liberating.

Sometimes, things can go very wrong, and it can feel impossible to find a way to the light – like walking through treacle whilst wearing wellington boots.

When you can find a blessing in the most awful of situations and circumstances, you start to take control of your destiny. It feels empowering.

When it becomes a habit, you know you've started the long journey home.

But first, you have to look with your mind, not your eyes. Close your eyes, go into yourself and look through the lens of unconditional love. You'll see more clearly.

Finding blessings in the most unexpected places is also a really nice way to live your life.

Exploring the Recurring Themes in this Book

In the 'Blessing bites' sections of this book, you'll see namaste hands. There's no single direct translation for the (originally Sanskrit) word 'namaste'; it's used as a salutation, often accompanied by a gesture. It's a truly beautiful word that expresses respect, appreciation and gratitude. As a salutation, it's both a greeting and a farewell, which can mean 'my spirit honours your spirit'.

This multipurpose word feels like the figure eight, which when laid sideways resembles the infinity symbol. If you say it quickly enough or repeat it, you can almost hear, "nice day," which is such a lovely thing to wish for yourself and others.

Namaste has multiple positive meanings and intentions. It's a goodwill word that honours the place in which one resides in the universe.

Regarding the gesture that often accompanies the word 'namaste', the hands come together at the heart to centre those thoughts, because this is where unconditional love can be felt for others as well as oneself. The practice transmits sincerity. 'Others' isn't restricted to human relationships, but it can apply to anything, both animate and inanimate.

However, self-appreciation and respect are vital for personal growth, to maintain healthy boundaries and in order to be true to yourself. When you're balanced and in harmony with life, you're in a better position to help and serve others.

Butterflies flit throughout and land on many of the pages of this book. These wonderful creatures teach us so much.

They're very relevant in the spiritual world because of the massive transformation they undergo. For most of us, becoming spiritual requires a huge change to become our true selves. We're reborn.

Butterflies give us hope. They inspire and motivate us. They're evidence of a wish fulfilled.

My dearest wish is that the caterpillar in you transforms into a beautiful and liberated butterfly, so you're able to lead a happy and true-to-yourself life.

Finally, one of the best ways to begin leading a more authentic life is to take action and identify your own blessings. You'll be amazed how many there are. So, I suggest you grab a notebook because there are a few places throughout the pages of this book where I encourage you to write down your blessings in disguise.

Introducing Gaia

Throughout this book, you'll come to know a character called Gaia, who strikes up conversations with various people and animals she meets whilst spending time on the beach.

Gaia is my higher or intuitive self. My inner guide, if you like. Her experiences are based on mine, but I see her as a universal figure, because I believe everything we need to live a happy life can be found within ourselves.

Gaia's conversations take place on a beach because this is the scene of my/her earliest memory, so it seems like a good location to discover blessings. In addition, the first topic discussed is Alzheimer's disease, a symptom of which is, sadly, memory loss. Sticking with the theme of memories, Gaia was also the name of the farm my parents owned in New South Wales, Australia. It was a place brimming with happy memories.

Gaia is another name for Mother Earth, by the way, and as this is something of a spiritual book, it seems to be the perfect name to give a central character.

I'll now let Gaia more thoroughly introduce herself to you.

Hi there!

I'm Gaia, and it's great to meet you, or *piacere* (pleasure to meet you), as they say in Italian. I'm showing off now.

During the first Covid-19 lockdown, I decided to learn the language that is, in my humble opinion, the most beautiful language on earth. It helped to keep me sane at a time when the world seemed to be falling apart. I'm half-Italian, so it also keeps me connected to my heritage – but I digress.

I have a truly amazing life: I have a wonderful family and friends; a gorgeous home; lots of interests; a job that I love; my dog, Daisy Boo, who is my best friend and constant companion; and money in the bank – and I've travelled the world.

But it wasn't always that way. Or rather it was, but I didn't always feel that great. That's because when bad things happened in life, as they do to all of us, it was sometimes hard to see my way through them and back to my happy place. I didn't always cope very well on the inside.

A whole lot of really, really, really bad, dark, heavy stuff happened to me, one thing after the other, and it went on for years. I was married to a chronic alcoholic, gambler, cheat, liar and thief who inflicted immense emotional and psychological abuse upon me. My mother was diagnosed with Alzheimer's and was eventually admitted to a care home. Her gradual deterioration took a terrible toll on my father.

During this time, for around a decade, I did a round trip of nearly 1,000 kilometres every few weeks – with my dog in tow

– to visit my parents to help care for them, both practically and emotionally, and offer support in any way I could.

My mother died of her illness in due course. I was getting ready to drive to the hospital to visit her when my family and I were contacted and told to get there sooner rather than later, as she'd taken a turn for the worse. She died before I could say goodbye, and this will always haunt me.

Against this backdrop, I was establishing a business. I was working extremely hard to build up a client base and earn a reputation, so I could earn a living.

I was also going through a very difficult early menopause, which left me feeling like a microwaved zombie.

There was also the constant worry about my sister's health. She was admitted to hospital periodically, and just as Covid-19 struck, she spent five weeks in intensive care.

Adding to my stress, a family member and I fell out over a private matter. It broke us both, but I'm glad to say we've since reconciled.

I was emotionally and physically exhausted all the time. I felt traumatised. My tank was empty. I didn't want to live any more.

But do you know what? They say it's darkest before the dawn, and from where I was, the only way I could go was up. A chance meeting with someone put me on the right path, and I slowly and painfully began my journey home – to get back to who I was and who I was always meant to be. It took about two and a half years to get to where I am today, and I'm still making changes to my life to free myself from what doesn't serve me.

And that's why I'm here: to show you there are blessings in bad things as well as in good things. Sometimes, you need to dig deep for them, like mining coal or opals.

It's easy to see what's in front of you when all is well, but when you're hurting, you can't always see what's there. Occasionally, you just have to close your eyes and be still – to think. That is, to use the most powerful thing you have: your mind.

The blessings are definitely there.

This book is for you. To help you, guide you and support you. To show you that you have the answers to your problems and the power to change unpleasant feelings for better ones.

There's a big lump of happiness inside you, and it starts with finding the blessings in adversity. Because if you can do that, you can do anything, be anything and have anything.

This is a safe place. I won't judge you. Take my hand, come with me and let me show you the way.

Venire. (Come.)

Blessings

Before you take that first sip of coffee

Hello again

I like to start my day with a steaming, big cup of posh coffee (i.e. not instant), but that's just me.

But did you ever think about the hundreds, if not thousands, of people who are responsible for getting that coffee into your cup? No, I didn't either until I started counting my blessings.

Here's who you need to thank before you take that first sip:

* Plantation owners
* Growers
* Pickers
* Packers
* Drivers and transporters
* Exporters and importers
* Merchant navy and air freight
* Coffee mills
* Coffee roasters
* Packaging people (the coffee has to be put in something)
* Advertising experts
* Coffee shops and supermarkets

* Consumers (let's face it, if you were the only person in the world who liked coffee, there wouldn't be any to drink because they wouldn't produce it just for you!)
* The maker of your mug (that's a whole other story!)

Saluti! (Cheers!)

Mmmmmmm.

After my coffee, I make time for myself – to just be. It's very important simply to sit in the moment and be me.

Sometimes, I like to go down to the sea to be me.

Blessing bites

- How you start your day is so important because everything you do should be a choice that's designed to make you feel good.
- How do you like to start your day? Do you make yourself a cup of tea or coffee? Do you pour yourself a juice or make a smoothie? Do you reach for a cereal packet, create a fruit salad or get a yoghurt out of the fridge?
- Perhaps you skip breakfast and do something else. Yoga? Listen to the news on the radio or watch it on TV? Walk the dog?
- It doesn't matter what your morning routine is, there will be someone to thank.
- Counting your blessings is a great way to start the day because it makes you feel warm and fuzzy inside, and it sets the tone for how your day could unfold. It's like having a protein shake before leaving the house.
  - Who are the people you could silently thank?
  - How does it make you feel to know that so many people/organisations are behind your morning routine?
  - Why should you feel blessed?

My earliest memory

Hi!

I was born by the sea. I love it. I love the drama of it. It can be as intense as a migraine one minute and as gentle as a whisper the next.

It has emotions, just like you and I do.

I love the aliveness of it; the way the salty air prickles my nose and invades my senses; the thunder of the waves surrendering to the shore; and the fizz of the foam celebrating its freedom.

The sea has been here *per sempre* (forever).

My earliest memory is of sitting on the sand, watching the last fingers of a wave creep up the shore to kiss my stubby, little baby toes. I had an awareness that I was wearing a pink-and-white checked bikini; that I had legs, feet and toes; and the brine was saying hello to me. It was funny, fun and mesmerising. I was only 18 months old.

This cherished memory is what I'm thinking about when someone breaks into my thoughts, like the waves steeling themselves to caress the sand.

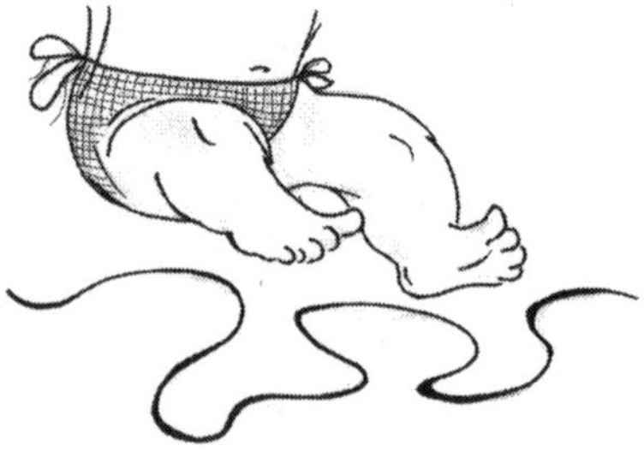

I wish my mum could remember things

Alba: "Is anyone sitting here?"

Gaia: "No, help yourself."

Alba: "Thanks. I'm Alba, by the way. I come here to think."

Gaia: "Me too. Not the name, that is. I mean, I come here to think as well. I'm Gaia."

Alba: "What were you thinking about?"

Gaia: "My earliest memory, actually, which just happens to be about the sea."

Alba: "Oh. That's nice. I wish my mum could remember things – such as her family. She's got Alzheimer's."

Gaia: "I'm so sorry. That's really tough on you and her."

Alba: "Yeah, it really is.

"Sometimes, she doesn't know who I am, and she looks at me with such vacant eyes. It's heartbreaking.

"But then, the other day, the care-home staff told me that Mum recognised my car when I pulled up in the car park. I've got a dark-blue Land Rover, like thousands of other people, but apparently, Mum said, 'That's my daughter's car,' and she waved at me through the window."

Gaia: "Hold on to that because that's a blessing. A small one, but a blessing, nonetheless. You'll remember that moment in years to come."

Alba: "I guess. It made my day, anyway."

Gaia: "This is going to sound a bit out there, but have you thought about what you have, rather than what you've lost or are losing?"

Alba: "*Cosa intendi?* [What do you mean?]"

Gaia: "That maybe there are some blessings somewhere in your awful situation."

Alba: "It's hard to see the blessings when your mum is dying and your family is going to pieces trying to cope."

Gaia: "I know, but sometimes, we have to use our imaginations to find peace. If you keep practising looking for the blessings, it'll become a habit. What you want also wants you.

"So, anger, resentment, guilt, frustration, shame and bitterness – all the things you're probably feeling – they're really big, heavy emotions. Like those rocks over there, they take up a lot of space.

"But if you clear them away, you make room for peace, joy, love, contentment and happiness, which feel so much better."

Alba: "How do I do that, and where do I start?"

Gaia: "It's easier said than done, I know, but give it a try and see if it makes a difference.

"You have the next few years to make some really special and unique memories with your mum. Spend as much time with her as possible – more than you would have otherwise, perhaps. Your mum is still here – physically, at least – so see if you can make the most of it.

"If she died suddenly, you wouldn't have a chance to say and do all the things you wanted to say and do, but never got around to. This way, you do have time. Don't waste it. Time is the most precious gift you can give to another person, whether they're aware of it or not."

Alba: "My parents have looked after me and supported me all my life. It's so painful to watch what's happening."

Gaia: "But you now have a chance to do for them what they've done for you. Care for your mum and support your dad. That's truly a gift.

"You're on a journey you didn't ask to take, but you'll meet people along the way, some of whom will stay in your life. They'll become your friends. And all because your mum got Alzheimer's."

Alba: "I guess it's better to know what she has than not know what we're dealing with."

Gaia: "You're getting the hang of it. Accept each moment with your mum as a gift. Just sit with her, holding her hand and singing songs together, because by some miracle, people with Alzheimer's seem to remember the words to songs.

"Listen to her ramblings. It really doesn't matter. Treat those tender moments like a kind of meditation, and practise being in the present moment. Just go along with it as best you can."

Alba: "Mum repeats herself a lot, and it drives us all mad. We try to be patient, but it's so hard sometimes."

Gaia: "When she's no longer able to speak properly or at all, you'll give anything to hear her repeat herself."

Alba: "I guess."

Gaia: "Count the blessings and the memories you and your mum have shared, but don't overlook the new memories you can create together."

Alba: "Mum can be quite funny and playful because she's regressed into childhood. That's when we laugh with her – never at her."

Gaia: "You've got a lot to be thankful for. If you were to focus on the stress, trauma and financial consequences of living with Alzheimer's – which is the reality – you'd go mad, and then you'd be no good whatsoever to your mum or your family.

"By looking for the blessings, even in the deepest and darkest of places, you stand a good chance of feeling better for a little while, and that has to be worth the effort."

Alba: "I'll think about it. *Grazie.* [Thank you.]"

Gaia: "*Di niente.* [Not at all.]"

Blessing bites

- When you need to remind yourself that your loved one is still there, recall those moments.
- As long as your loved one is alive, you have the opportunity to focus on what you have, rather than what you've lost or are losing.
- Sometimes, we have to use our imaginations to find peace.
- The more you practise using your imagination, the easier it gets. It becomes a habit.
- What you want also wants you.
- Clear away heavy, negative feelings to make space for lighter, more positive ones, because it feels so much better.
- Make some really special and unique memories whilst you can.
- Spend as much time together as possible because the inevitable will happen one day. When it does, at least you'll be able to look back and say you made the most of the time you had left.
- Time is the most precious gift you can give to another person, whether they're aware of it or not.

- You now have a chance to help and support your mum, dad or other family members in the same way they once did for you. You can return the favour – that truly is a gift!
- You're on a journey you didn't ask to take, but you'll meet some amazing people along the way.
- It's better to know what you're dealing with than not.
- Practise being in the present moment and just go with the flow as best you can.
- Don't overlook the new memories you can create together.
- Your tank needs to be full before you can help others.
- Finding the blessings in dark places can help you feel better, if only for a little while, and that has to be worth the effort.

I was determined to escape to another country

by Alan Brett

Liphook | Hampshire | England

Let me begin by saying that, yes, blessings can come out of adversity quite spontaneously, sometimes almost immediately and sometimes much later. They can also arise either consciously or subconsciously, by choice of action.

In my early childhood, during the Second World War, I was in Malta throughout the siege. It was a period of massive adversity that, in the mind of a child, wasn't perceived as such. I was simply excited and fascinated with watching dive bombers dropping their deadly loads. I was equally fascinated when watching planes that had been shot by artillery spiral down vertically into the sea.

It was only as an adult that I perceived the danger and adversity. No blessings came out of that, but it was a catalyst for subsequent events much later, from which blessings did emerge.

My father died during the war, and by the time I was 11 years old and back in England, my mother had remarried. That was the worst period of my entire life. It was adversity in its most extreme manifestation.

My stepfather was a violent paedophile. I was never called by my name – I was always 'Boy'. Apart from frequent sexual abuse, I was also subjected to beatings. One in particular that's seared in my memory was when I was made to take off my pyjamas and then severely horsewhipped.

Now this is where my own intervention ultimately resulted in blessings to come. They didn't arise spontaneously, but significantly, they did come to me.

I was determined to escape to another country, and I found that I could go to Australia, where I didn't know anyone, but I had to wait until I was 16. My mother signed her consent as soon as I reached that age, but it wasn't over yet. Once in Australia, I discovered that I'd been recruited as cheap labour and was paid a quarter of the rate paid to Australian boys.

So adversity continued until, once again, my actions triggered a response that brought me the blessings I hadn't expected, but nevertheless, I received them in abundance.

I ran off and joined a cattle-and-sheep-droving outfit run by two brothers. To this very day, those were the happiest years of my life. I lived outdoors, slept in a wagon and worked with horses, which I loved. I had many exciting adventures, was well paid and had the greatest friends I could wish for. Also, as part of the process of assimilation into this new and appealing culture, I took up rodeo, riding buckjump horses and wild bulls. I made several more great friends as a result, and I was totally fulfilled. So out of adversity came my greatest blessings.

But more was to come. Whilst in hospital for a few days, I read about the adventures of working as a cadet medical patrol officer in New Guinea. This appealed to me, and having applied and been accepted, my blessings out of the original adversity continued, as I enjoyed the adventure of working amongst people who were still immersed in a Stone Age culture.

Three years later, I returned to Australia to go to university, and I met and married a pretty, young girl who was half-Italian and half-Slovenian. I wouldn't say that I entered a period of adversity – that would be too strong a word – but we did have our difficulties.

Again, it was as a result of my own choices that I found myself having to work in the city, which I hated, but out of that came two blessings: my two little girls and the family I had always longed for.

But blessings can arise out of adversity, be lost and then be regained.

My wife wanted to live in another country, and I wanted to farm and get back to horses. Together, we found a way out of what could have been an impasse. So again, blessings arose out of this difficult time when we found a lovely, small family farm back in England, where we were both happy with what we had. We also had the pleasure of seeing our daughters so happy with their horses and ponies.

Then, without going into detail, adversity began to creep in once more, and blessings became ephemeral. Adversity and blessings became intertwined.

Finally, we were settled once again, and apart from the inevitable periods of turbulence that afflict every relationship, the decision to spend our final years in Wales turned out to be a blessing. We found very good friends and loved the Welsh culture.

Then came a massive blow, as my wife was diagnosed with Alzheimer's. So I was deeply back into adversity again, with the trauma of caring for someone with dementia. With very little help available and her finally passing away, adversity took its toll on me.

But even out of this adversity, blessings came to me. I rediscovered the healing power of poetry. I'd written poetry over many years, but now it was different.

When at times I felt despair,
I found tools that would repair.

Poetry gave me the key
To find myself in me.

I had my blessings, but paid my due,
And so you'll find it is with you.

Cucciolo

Gaia: "Hey, you're a little cutie. What's your name?"

Cucciolo: "Cucciolo. It means 'puppy' in Italian. I'm not cute, by the way; I'm a teenager, and my name is rubbish for my street cred."

Gaia: "It's a lovely name, and your parents chose it because they love you."

Cucciolo: "What do you mean?"

Gaia: "If they didn't love you, they wouldn't have given you a name."

Cucciolo: "I'd rather not have a name than have something that people make fun of."

Gaia: "What other people think of your name is none of your business. Worrying about what others think is a wasted emotion.

"Have you got a nice, soft, warm bed?"

Cucciolo: "One in the kitchen, two in the living room and, as a treat, I can go upstairs on special occasions."

Gaia: "There you go. Are you fed every day, and do you have plenty of fresh water?"

Cucciolo: "Of course."

Gaia: "Do your mum and dad take you for nice walks? Do they take lots of photos of you and post them on Facebook and Instagram, so everyone can see their fur baby? Do they take you to the vet for your vaccinations and your worm and flea treatments?"

Cucciolo: "Well, yeah."

Gaia: "I see you're wearing a nice collar with a name tag. What's engraved on it?"

Cucciolo: "My name, address and phone number."

Gaia: "That's so if you get lost or wander off, like now, your parents can get you back. Because you're part of the family."

Cucciolo: "Yes, but I want a big boy's name."

Gaia: "A name doesn't make you big. What's inside you is what matters. Be true to yourself and kind to others. That's what makes you big and will set you apart from others as you journey through life.

"You have comfy beds, food, water, toys, walks and medicine.

"It's OK to dislike your name, but don't lose sight of what really counts.

"When you're old and with a grey muzzle, you'll be glad you were given a cute, young name such as Cucciolo."

Cucciolo: "I s'pose."

Blessing bites

- Your name was chosen with love and care by people who love and care for you.
- What other people think of your name, or anything else about you, is none of your business.
- Worrying about what others think is a wasted emotion.
- When someone gives you things to make you comfortable, warm, safe and happy, it means they love you and care about you.
- A name doesn't make you big.
- What's inside you is what matters.
- Be true to yourself and kind to others.
- Don't lose sight of what really counts.

My illness has made me better in a lot of ways

by Anita Lenzo

Sydney | New South Wales | Australia

I've had my share of challenges because my mental health was so poor. I have bipolar.

I believe I've suffered so much that something has happened to my personality. I'm kinder, more caring and have double doses of empathy. My suffering has acted as a springboard to make me a better human being. I believe I was already a caring person, but the mental health problems I've experienced have made me even more so and have enhanced those traits.

Also, as much as I care about others, I've realised that I need to put myself first.

I've always had faith in something bigger than myself. I think that's how I survived.

I was utilising law-of-attraction techniques[1] in my twenties, but I somehow forgot to use it beyond that, until I reached my late forties. In the last few years, I've manifested a lot of good experiences, as well as some treasured possessions.

---

1. The law of attraction is a philosophy in which positive thoughts bring positive experiences and results into a person's life, whilst negative thoughts bring negative experiences and results.

So, in a nutshell, my illness has made me better in a lot of ways and has enhanced my ability to see myself, in the sense that I'm keenly self-aware. The benefit of being like this is that I know who I am because I've needed to dig deep to survive. Most of the time, I wanted to die, as I was so depressed and in enormous amounts of pain.

Now, however, I lead an authentic life because my intuition is heightened and I know who I am.

Losing my dream job was the best thing that ever happened to me

Liberty: "It's happened twice now."

Gaia: "What has?"

Liberty: "Losing my dream job or not getting the job of my dreams in the first place."

Gaia: "Sorry to hear that."

Liberty: "Don't be. Something better came along instead. Much, much better, in fact.

"The first time it happened, I was overjoyed when I was offered a job that I'd wanted for years. It was a dream come true. I felt on top of the world, like I could fly and like my heart would burst with happiness."

Gaia: "That sounds amazing. So what happened?"

Liberty: "Just a few months later, I was made redundant. There were cutbacks, and it was a case of 'last one in, first one out'. It felt so unfair. It was like a cruel joke, and my whole world came crashing down."

Gaia: "That sucks. Talk about heartbreaking!"

Liberty: "It was. I cried buckets. I became depressed, and I felt angry, resentful and full of self-pity.

"I seemed to be the only one who cared about how I felt, so after a while, I thought, *What can I do to change the way I feel and to make things better?*

"I was wasting my energy on mourning the loss of something I couldn't change, but I could alter the way I reacted to what had happened."

Gaia: "That's very grown-up of you."

Liberty: "Maybe. I don't know. I just got sick of feeling awful all the time and pretending to be happy when I wasn't."

Gaia: "So what did you do?"

Liberty: "I moved halfway around the world."

Gaia: "That's a bit drastic!"

Liberty: "Not for me. I was born in Australia, and I have family there, so I thought I'd go home, see everyone and see if I could get back my dream job, but in a new place."

Gaia: "*E*? [And?]"

Liberty: "And everything fell into place. In fact, I got a better job with better career prospects and loads more money. I was *molto contento* [very happy]."

Gaia: "I'm pleased for you, but most people can't or won't go to those lengths to make things better."

Liberty: "They don't have to. They just have to think differently and then take action – as in, do something about it. I could have saved myself so much heartache and trauma if only I'd seen things in a different way at the time.

"I needed to consider things such as *Why did this bad thing happen to me? Is there a reason for it? Can I learn from it? Are there any good bits? Can I do something about it? Is there something better around the corner? What's the Universe trying to tell me?*"

Gaia: "Well, good for you. So what happened the second time?"

Liberty: "*Scusi*? [Pardon?]"

Gaia: "You said you lost your dream job twice. Did you go all the way to Australia only to lose that job too?"

Liberty: "No, not at all. I moved up the career ladder and was very successful for many years. But then, I wanted a particular, very niche job, and I tried so hard to get it."

Gaia: "What did you do?"

Liberty: "I chased it. I kept in touch with the boss. I kept reminding him that I was still here and sent him regular updates of my work. He was always very kind, but he never took the next step to actually employ me.

"I pursued this job relentlessly, and what happens when you chase something?"

Gaia: "It runs a mile."

Liberty: "Exactly. Looking back, I tried way too hard and came across as desperate. I thought the only way I could ever be happy would be if I got that job. That was a mistake, but I'd become obsessed.

"I wasted so much time and effort trying to impress people when they didn't really care."

Gaia: "That happens when you don't have healthy boundaries."

Liberty: "Tell me about it! But a magical thing happened when I gave up on ever getting this job. I got a call one day, totally out of the blue, asking me to go to a meeting to discuss a position in a completely different industry, but one still using my skills.

"It was for a job I never would have considered once, and in fact, I nearly turned down the request for a meeting."

Gaia: "But you didn't?"

Liberty: "No, thank goodness. I went for the interview. I got the job, and it turned out to be the best job I've ever had, with the best boss I've ever had and bringing in the most money I've ever earned.

"I met some amazing people and did some phenomenal things that I never would have otherwise. My standards went sky-high because I was working with such exceptionally talented and clever people. And you become like the people you spend your time with.

“That job, my biggest adventure, set me up for the rest of my life. I’ll always be grateful for it.”

Gaia: “I love a happy ending.”

Liberty: “Me too. If I’d got the other job I chased for so long, I wouldn’t be where I am today.

“I feel so blessed, and I believe the Universe was guiding me.”

Gaia: “Amen.”

Blessing bites

- Something better often comes along when you least expect it.
- When you feel angry, resentful and full of self-pity, the only person you're hurting is yourself.
- You have the power to change the way you feel and make yourself feel better.
- Don't waste your energy on things you can't change. Change the way you react to bad or difficult things instead.
- You don't have to go to extraordinary lengths to improve your life and turn a difficult situation around. You just have to think differently and take action.
- You can save yourself a lot of heartache and trauma by looking at things in a different way.
- Ask yourself the following:
  - Why did this bad thing happen to me?
  - Is there a reason for it?
  - Can I learn from it?
  - Are there any good bits?
  - Can I do something about it?

- Is something better around the corner?
- What is the Universe trying to tell me?”

- When you’re too attached to an outcome and chase it relentlessly, it runs in the opposite direction.
- Happiness comes from within.
- Don’t waste time and effort trying to impress people who don’t really care and never will.
- Cultivate and maintain healthy boundaries.
- Your standards are significantly raised when you work with talented and clever people. They lift you up.
- You become like the people you spend your time with.

I prayed to God for help to find a woman who would love me for who I am

by Salvador Jimenez

Hampshire | England

Hi, my name is Salvador. In my experience of life, nothing is coincidence.

When I was 24 years old, I got married, and there were always difficult times. This woman never loved me. I was always praying to God to help me find a woman who would love me for who I am.

I was born in Guadalajara and was living in Mexico at this time. I always had faith that, one day, I'd find the love of my life.

I'm a musician, and I had a dream to travel around the world, but my reality at that time was horrible. Every day, my wife and I were fighting. It continued like this for nine years until something happened unexpectedly. A French entertainment company was in Mexico looking for a band to perform in Hong Kong. I thought, *This is the opportunity I've been waiting for*, and so I got divorced and decided to have a new adventure on the other side of the planet.

I went to Hong Kong, and I met the most kind, beautiful and wonderful woman named Jane. When I met her for the first time, she seemed like an angel. She gave me the most beautiful smile. She gave me hope. She taught me how to live. She taught me how to be happy. She showed me how to be me. But the funny thing was that I didn't speak English, and she didn't speak Spanish.

I think that, on this Planet Earth, you always have a way to be happy and to be whatever you want. Just open your eyes, open your mind, open your heart and see what you want inside you.

I know it isn't easy, but I promise you that it isn't impossible to be happy.

My life path changed twice to bring me to my beautiful soul mate

by Jane Brett de Jimenez
Hampshire | England

I actually have two stories, which are linked, that reveal several blessings in disguise, and they inadvertently led to the best and biggest events in my life: a huge adventure – the stuff of movies – and meeting my beloved soul mate. I travelled a convoluted path, but all obstacles, disappointments, twists and turns led me to where I needed to be.

It was the end of May 1991 when I graduated from the Lanarkshire College of Midwifery. Having been unable to secure a midwifery job in Scotland, a country I'd fallen head over heels in love with, I temporarily moved in with my grandmother in Wiltshire.

I'd previously visited a fortune teller, who'd said that I'd work in a large town, and she could see cobblestones. I decided that it must be Oxford, as I'd seen an advert in the *Nursing Times* for my dream job, which was in the maternity unit at the John Radcliffe Hospital.

Imagine the shock and disappointment I felt when, after my interview, I was told I hadn't got the job. I was devastated.

My grandmother, who was very wise, suggested I look at doing something else that I might like until the right job came along. I went along with what she said, and I trawled through the pages of various nursing magazines. Midwifery jobs were as rare as hens' teeth, but I didn't fancy working on medical or surgical wards any more. I was a midwife now.

I found an advert for work in a neonatal intensive care unit (NICU) and that interested me. It was something I'd contemplated doing before doing my midwifery training, so I thought I might as well apply.

I called, and an interview was arranged. I was nervous and excited at the same time. I have to admit, though, my heart wasn't fully in it, as I wanted to work as a midwife. I didn't make a huge effort during the interview, and my interviewers commented that I was the only person to turn up in a miniskirt!

However, that evening, I received a call informing me that the job was mine, and I could start the following Monday. I couldn't believe it! I'd actually been offered a job, and the fact that it wasn't as a midwife didn't seem to matter any more. I told the person who called that I didn't think I'd get the job after the miniskirt comment, and they said they liked my 'funkiness'. I've been described as many things in my time, but 'funky' was never one of them – though I did quite like it!

I started working in the NICU at Leicester Royal Infirmary – and by the way, the town centre has some cobbled streets. I took to the job like a duck to water, and I absolutely loved it. My colleagues, the work and everything about it made me feel alive. It was the best move I'd ever made, and I was so happy.

It was such a massive blessing that I didn't get that midwifery job in Oxford after all.

Whilst in Leicester, I did a diploma in the Special and Intensive Care of the Newborn. About halfway through the course, we had an elective week in which we could spend time at another NICU anywhere in the world. Most people went back to their home cities or to London. I wanted to go to the USA and work in New York or Miami, so I visited the medical school library to search for hospitals that had nice names. There was no internet in those days.

I wrote to six hospitals, and four responded: three were in New York and the other was in Miami. The New York hospitals required a range of vaccinations, but the Miami one only required a measles, mumps and rubella (MMR) vaccination, which was much easier. That's how I decided I'd go to Miami for a week and work in the neonatal unit at Mount Sinai Hospital, Miami Beach.

The hospital was great and, as the address suggests, right on the beach. I also spent a day at Jackson Memorial Hospital, which is a huge public hospital with a large emergency room, and it's the state's main trauma centre. At the time, the massive NICU at Jackson Memorial Hospital was spread over four floors. This was the dream for me; real cutting-edge stuff happened there. My mind was all over the place with excitement.

The unit manager at Jackson Memorial Hospital even offered me a job after I declared that I'd love to work there. She said that, once I'd finished my diploma, I'd need to do the USA conversion exams and the Florida state exams. I was so excited, and I had my whole future mapped out in front of me.

Once I was back in the UK, I was still very excited and started planning a timeline to achieve what I needed to work back in Florida.

Meanwhile, students from the adult ICU course spent a couple of weeks with us neonatal bods, and we mentored them during their time on the NICU. One day, I was mentoring Christina – a lovely girl with a bright and shiny personality – and together, we transferred a baby back to his original hospital. We got talking about what we were going to do when we finished the course, and I told her about the wonderful Jackson Memorial Hospital and my dream of working there. I then asked Christina about her plans.

She said, "I'm going backpacking around the world for a year."

I was silent for a moment. Hadn't this once been my dream? A dream that I'd buried, but which was now rising to the surface. Suddenly, I found myself telling her to forget everything I'd just told her – I was joining her on her trip.

About six months went by. I was still enjoying working in the NICU, I'd found a new boyfriend and was enjoying my life. Then, one day, Christina knocked on my door and said that we needed to start thinking about getting ourselves sorted for our adventure. OMG, this was real now. We sat and chatted about the itineraries, vaccinations, clothes and equipment we needed to get organised. The excitement was overwhelming. I was ready to burst.

A few months after that, we finally left for the biggest and greatest adventure of our lives. My mind still often goes back to this fantastic, wonderful, beautiful, fabulous, carefree time of my life.

We travelled for more than a year, and were nowhere near the end of our trip when we arrived in Hong Kong, almost penniless. We'd each have to get a job! We'd thought perhaps waitressing or working in a bar, until a bloke at the hostel suggested that, as nurses, we could work at one of the hospitals. It would certainly be better paid than waiting on tables. With just a few pounds left on our credit cards, we bought some interview clothes, and it wasn't long before we both secured work at the Hong Kong Adventist Hospital: Christina in the cardio-pulmonary lab, and me in midwifery.

Our intention was to stay for a year, save hard and continue with our travels. However, 12 months later, neither of us was ready to leave Hong Kong, so we looked for a better flat to live in instead.

About 18 months after that, I had the opportunity to work for six weeks in Tianjin, China, not far from the capital, Beijing. I was contracted to work for the expat population of a multinational company, providing Western-style healthcare. Six weeks turned into 14 months. I loved every second of it and made some fabulous local friends too.

I also met an American woman who promised me a job as the director of nursing at a private American hospital that was yet to be built. When my contract in Tianjin had come to an end, I took a holiday, visited my parents in the UK and kept in touch with this woman. But with no sign of the hospital materialising, I cut my losses and returned to Hong Kong, where I was very happy.

One of my friends, a Chinese man, became my boyfriend, but he wasn't what I really wanted. I'd had many boyfriends, but I was tired of men being so problematic, so demanding and treating me like a bank. I decided that if I couldn't find a man who was kind, thoughtful, sweet and generous, and who would love me for who I am, I didn't want one. For the first time in my life, I was happy at the thought of being single forever.

Typically, not long after that, I met my soul mate, Salvador – a Mexican mariachi. We met at a salsa class. He and his band mates were friends with my salsa teacher. They joined in the dance class, and at the end, I saw Salvador and decided to speak to him. But before I reached him, I overheard someone ask him if he spoke English to which he replied, "No." So, I decided that, as I can't speak Spanish, we wouldn't be able to communicate, and then I went home.

A couple of weeks later, Salvador approached me at a nightclub and asked me to dance. I accepted, and we did. Then, Salvador walked off and returned with an American woman who spoke Spanish and English. Through her, he asked me to teach him English and he offered to teach me Spanish in return. It sounded great, but unfortunately, at that time, I was going to work in South Korea for two weeks.

When I returned from Seoul, we met up – me with a Spanish–English dictionary and Salvador with a thing that looked like a calculator, but which translated words. We sat together for hours, putting the world to rights. Initially, we didn't know each other's languages, but we managed to talk about movies, news, politics, our countries and life in general.

Before long, we were smitten with each other, and not long afterwards, I told my friends that Salvador would be the last boyfriend I'd ever have. That was in March 1998, and we've been together ever since.

We've learned each other's language, lived together and got married. We've had a magical life together. We're still going strong and are still very much in love after all these years. He's my true soul mate.

So, my life path changed twice to bring me to my beautiful soul mate. The first time was when I went travelling with Christina instead of moving to Miami. The second time was when I returned to Hong Kong after my stint in China.

There have been so many twists and turns, and so many things I badly wanted to come to fruition that didn't, but all those initial disappointments turned out to be blessings in disguise, because my life has been a ball and is so much richer for the experiences I've had.

But most of all, what I thought were disappointments were really hidden blessings because I met the man of my dreams.

Blessings in lockdown

Well, hello...

Firstly, let me make it crystal clear that I don't believe there are any blessings to be had from someone having Covid-19. The pandemic has killed millions of people around the world, and it continues to rob people of their lives and quality of life. For every person who dies, dozens of people are left heartbroken or adversely affected in some way: family, friends, neighbours, employers, colleagues and communities.

However, one of the consequences of Covid-19 – lockdown – has revealed some unexpected blessings, and it's those I prefer to dwell on:

1. Lockdown gave people more time, particularly with loved ones, because either they worked from home or they had more time to keep in touch by phone or video chats.

2. Having more time on their hands meant people fixed things in their own home that they'd never got around to before because life got in the way.

3. People had the time and inclination to learn a language. *Buongiorno*! (Good morning!)

   I know a chap who decided to learn Japanese so that he could speak to his future grandchildren. Brilliant!

4. People took advantage of opportunities to master technology, which in turn helped them to stay in touch with family and friends. Learning how to use technology properly is never going to be wasted.

5. There was less pollution due to less industrial activity, and also because there were fewer cars on the road, planes in the sky and trains on the tracks.

6. People rediscovered nature. Bliss. Those who were lucky enough to have parks, fields and beaches nearby were able to spend more time communing with nature, which is something I think has been lost to many people these days.

7. People cleaned their homes because they had the time and it gave them something to do. It was like a really good spring clean. Show me a house that doesn't need one!

8. People learned what helped them to cope with the hardships of lockdown, because if you can benefit your mental health during a pandemic, you have a new coping tool you can use in other areas of your life when things get tough.

9. People got to know their neighbours, or got to know them better, by offering to help. This was especially important where elderly neighbours were concerned,

because many needed assistance with shopping, getting prescriptions picked up or running errands.

10. People got fit. They suddenly had time to lose a few kilos without moving from their living room. There was plenty of help and advice online regarding this, if they weren't able to get outside for a walk or run.

11. People read – *lots*!

12. Many people turned to DIY. There's always going to be something in your home/garden that needs attention.

13. After burning some calories with an online keep-fit class, people experimented with new recipes. *Buon apetito.* (Enjoy your meal.)

14. Community spirit really came to the fore. This was a biggie. People truly pulled together to help each other and volunteer assistance. A friend of mine is a dressmaker who makes amazing wedding dresses, but, of course, weddings stopped during the pandemic. Many other dressmakers also lost their jobs at this time. My friend wanted to do something useful with her time, so she set up a Facebook group for those who could make scrubs and masks for the NHS and care-home staff. This was all done for free by the volunteers – they donated their time, and the materials were donated too.

15. Fundraisers popped up everywhere. Look no further than Captain Sir Tom Moore, but there were many, many others just like him who made a big difference in their own small way.

16. Meditation. Lockdown was a great trigger for learning to meditate. It's great for good mental health and getting in touch with your inner self. That, by the way, isn't some woo-woo phrase. Your inner or metaphysical self is where happiness and fulfilment resides.

    What happens in your inner world is reflected in your outer world. You don't believe me? Learn to meditate, get in touch with who you are and see what happens.

17. People made playlists of their favourite songs, and then danced to them to keep fit!

18. Others learned a new hobby or rediscovered a former one.

19. New businesses were born. They say necessity is the mother of invention, and so it is.

20. Colds and flu were almost non-existent because clean hands were back in fashion and sanitising was so important in the fight against Covid-19.

21. People slept better or for longer or both. Having more time meant more time to sleep too.
22. Break-ups and divorces increased in number. Yes, divorce. Lockdown forced people to live in a confined space for a long period of time. For some, this resulted in them calling time on their marriage or relationship.

Why's that a good thing? Well, it appears the pandemic was the perfect storm for couples who may have already been on shaky ground. It acted as a catalyst for break-ups that were likely to happen anyway.

Speaking of divorce, we're going to talk about that after the next story.

We were surviving the Covid-19 pandemic like those little wild flowers that survive in the most difficult places

by Amparo Gabela

Quito | Ecuador

Rumours were heard everywhere on the news. A virus had started to spread throughout the world.

In March 2020, we were pressured by the government and its measures to contain the Covid-19 virus and avoid massive propagation. Airports and borders throughout the world started to close, and Ecuador followed these restrictions, leaving us secluded from the world.

As a tour guide, I had to act quickly and find a way to help my tourists leave the country and reach their homes. The situation was full of uncertainties, and we didn't have answers to their questions. We just had to do our work and follow protocols. Thankfully, all of them arrived safely in their home countries.

I went home and locked myself inside with my son, Felipe. Everything in Ecuador was closed except the supermarkets. We'd never faced this kind of situation in our lives.

Life stopped abruptly, the days passed and the anguish grew, as did the fear of what we were facing. There was no topic of conversation other than how many people were passing away due to the virus.

The tourism industry around the world was frozen, and as a freelance tour guide, my despair started to increase because I didn't have work or an income. Not having a job and asking ourselves, "How are we going to live?" increased our despair.

People who lost their jobs around the country started small entrepreneurships or left the country. I found myself in a very delicate position where I couldn't find something to do, as I tend to limit myself due to my age.

Felipe was studying his fifth semester of finance at Universidad San Francisco de Quito (USFQ). At the same time, he motivated me to start painting again.

The plan was to create watercolour paintings of the diverse flowers from Ecuador and sell them online. We decided to start an Instagram profile named @7_malas_hierbas to promote the art pieces I was creating. I was in charge of producing an original painting each day, and Felipe was in charge of obtaining followers and checking analytics. We were surviving the pandemic like those little wildflowers that survive in the most difficult places and whose beauty shines constantly.

Even though I've painted throughout my whole life, I've never been exposed to such a broad audience. Felipe was reaching people around the world through paid ads. Some of his ads were reaching more than 20,000 people.

I had to start mastering my painting skills and perfecting my style. We started selling art pieces nationally and internationally in 10 countries.

Throughout those months, we decided to add new products, such as bookmarks and personalised paintings. We perfected the social media posts too, and we began to include stories in each post of the day, so that people would stay interested in our products.

With this small business, Felipe was able to pay for his college education and our other necessities.

We noticed that, even though people were closed in their houses, they wanted to acquire art. Art is a significant expression of our existence. It's what makes us human.

I'm extremely grateful for the position I find myself in, and I'll continue to pursue this artistic career and reach more places around the globe.

I had a stone in my shoe

Gaia: "You look like you're running away from something."

Manna: "I'm running *to* something."

Gaia: "Wow. Where are you heading?"

Manna: "To freedom. My new life. I'm running home."

Gaia: "What do you mean?"

Manna: "I'm divorcing my husband, and I feel so happy, light and at peace now I've made the decision to leave."

Gaia: "Good for you."

Manna: "It took a long time. He's an alcoholic, and I kept making excuses for him. I kept hoping he'd change. Then, I started changing myself because he made me feel that his boozing – and the consequences of it – were all my fault."

Gaia: "It's called 'denial.'"

Manna: "I made myself small so that he could feel big, and I'm mad at myself for doing that.

"Looking back, I gave so much of myself away that there was nothing left for me."

Gaia: "You gave away your power. Big mistake."

Manna: "Yep. I grieved the death of my marriage – and the death of who I was – for years, but everything is different now. I've emerged from my chrysalis to become a beautiful butterfly."

Gaia: "Sadly, pain and suffering are often necessary for positive transformation."

Manna: "I had an expectation that wasn't met. That's how I choose to see things."

Gaia: "That's very profound."

Manna: "I did a lot of work on myself and had a spiritual awakening. I know now that your inner world reflects your outer world.

"I had to change how I thought and felt about things before my reality changed. When things inside me shifted, things outside me shifted too – for the better."

Gaia: "Emotion is energy in motion. When you change a negative feeling to a positive one, you start moving in the right direction."

Manna: "That's exactly what happened. How did you know that?"

Gaia: "I've been where you are. When you find yourself and it gives you the courage to take action, it's the most liberating feeling in the world."

Manna: "Manna from heaven!"

Gaia: "*Essatamente.* [Exactly.]

"But the Universe had to break you first to show you why it created you. You had to go through what you experienced so you could come out the other end and live authentically."

Manna: "I had a stone in my shoe, and I had to take it out to continue my journey.

"I could sit here and tell you about all the horrible things my husband did to me. I could also tell you how I contributed to them by enabling his behaviour.

"But instead, I'm going to celebrate the blessings that have come from my divorce."

Gaia: "Freedom! You can do what you want, when you want, where you want and with whom you want. No more fitting in, giving in, giving up, making do or doing without. No more unmet needs."

Manna: "New beginnings! A big adventure awaits me because I'm starting afresh with a clean slate. A new town, a new home and a new job. A new life. I'm so excited; it'll be so much fun."

Gaia: "New friends too. I don't know about you, but I've found that some of the people whom I thought would be there for me were conspicuous by their absence, whilst other people appeared out of nowhere to hold and support me."

Manna: "Oh yeah. That's so true. Divorce is a great opportunity to review your friendships and keep only those who are there for you."

Gaia: "Empowerment! Divorce is often the catalyst for doing things you didn't find the courage to do previously. This is when you learn who you really are and become the true you. You find your soul's path."

Manna: "Happy! Positive energy minus toxic behaviour equals more joy."

Gaia: "I'll take that any day.

"And weight loss! There's nothing like divorce to get rid of those excess kilos."

Manna: "That, and my eating habits have changed now I'm on my own. No more cooking every night if I don't feel like it or eating food I don't particularly enjoy, just to fit in."

Gaia: "Well, I wish you all the best. Something tells me you're going to be OK.

"You're making space for better things to come into your life, and that includes people. There are people looking for someone just like you, but they won't find you unless you start walking towards them."

Manna: "Or running."

Blessing bites

- Getting divorced doesn't have to be depressing.
- Divorce can bring freedom and a new life. It's a chance to wipe the slate clean and start again.
- You'll feel so happy, light and at peace when you make the decision to leave someone who's not right for you.
- If you're the one being left, you'll eventually feel happy, light and at peace too. It might just take a little longer.
- Don't keep making excuses for bad behaviour.
- You're not responsible for how someone else behaves or the consequences of it.
- Don't expect people to change. They don't and won't.
- Don't change who you are fundamentally just to fit in with somebody else.
- If somebody doesn't love and respect you the way you are, walk away.
- Don't make yourself small so that someone else can feel big.
- If someone can't feel big without making you feel small, it's their problem, and it shouldn't ever become your problem.

Blessing bites

- When you give too much of yourself, you give away your power.
- When you realise the mistake of giving too much, you can begin the process of changing from a caterpillar into a beautiful butterfly.
- Pain and suffering are often necessary for positive transformation to happen.
- Your inner world reflects your outer world.
- You have to change how you think and feel about things before your reality will change.
- When things inside you shift, things outside you shift too.
- Emotion is energy in motion.
- Change a negative feeling to a positive one, and you'll start moving in the right direction.
- When you find the courage to take action, you'll feel so liberated. It'll spur you on to keep going.
- Sometimes, you have to reach breaking point and crack open before change occurs and you can start living authentically.
- Divorce means new adventures – often a new home, job, friends and waistline!

- It can feel empowering to learn who you truly are.
- Divorce makes space for better things in your life, including people.
- There are people looking for someone just like you, but you have to start walking towards them.

A car crash led to a new life

by Dr Pamela Schulz OAM

Adelaide | South Australia | Australia

It was New Year's Eve in 1973, and I'd completed a long shift at a notorious youth detention centre.

The next morning, a dear mate picked me up to drive me to my parents' house for lunch and to celebrate the new year. I was living with them in between getting a divorce and studying for a certificate in child development at the University of Adelaide in South Australia.

I was only 27 years old and scared about my future, but I was hopeful that further study and public sector employment would garner a future for me and my children, who were currently with their male biological parent. My ex-husband was a rich and powerful surgeon, and hard to take to task, so this enforced separation of me and my children was predictable.

As I was saying, at 10am on New Year's Day, my mate Michael picked me up. He had a lovely bottle of Great Western Australian sparkling wine in the boot of his car to take to my mum and dad.

En route, at the corner of two main roads, a drunken driver – who had no doubt been celebrating the night before – ran a red light and directly hit the passenger side of the little sports car my friend and I were travelling in, where I was sitting. This led to significant damage to both me and the car.

When the emergency services arrived, it was ascertained that I had no feeling in my legs and my long, dark hair was entangled in the wreckage. After what seemed like ages, the paramedics finally cut my hair to loosen it from the tangled metal and then placed me on a spinal board. I was rushed to the Royal Adelaide Hospital, where it was found that I had several fractured vertebrae.

I couldn't feel my feet initially, but that changed as the weeks wore on. I was eventually discharged from hospital, with medication and strict instructions about bed rest and lifting things.

My dear friend Annie insisted on taking me to Murray Bridge, a river town about 75 kilometres from Adelaide, to stay at her brother's dairy farm, where I'd eat fresh food and take in the fresh air to speed up my recovery.

During my stay, in the week that followed the Australia Day long weekend, hay carting took place on the farm, and strapping, good-looking men were in abundance.

I noticed one of them and asked Annie, "Who is the dark-brown, auburn-haired Omar Sharif lookalike?"

"Oh," she said, "that's just Schulzie. All the girls are after him, and besides, I think he's a bit younger than you, so eyes right, please!"

Later that day, a fundraiser took place for rural youth, and I was asked to read fortunes with cards as Madame Zara. I'd learned this from my mother as a party trick, which often pleased people. The young man, now known to me as Roy, approached and asked for his fortune to be told. I predicted that he'd go overseas with a grey-haired woman in the next 6 to 12 weeks.

Everyone laughed, but he said, "Listen, guys. I booked the tickets yesterday. I'm taking my mother to New Zealand to meet up with my long-lost older brother."

After that, I was busy all afternoon!

I also predicted that Roy would get married that year to a dark-haired woman who'd been born overseas. Little did I know that it was me!

Later that day, Roy asked if I'd like to go to the football cabaret in town. I said I'd be delighted. When he came to pick me up, he arrived with a lovely, black walking stick with an orchid attached. It was so thoughtful and complemented my black frock.

I did warn him, though, that I couldn't negotiate stairs or steps yet, as I was still rehabilitating.

He replied, "This will be a first, carrying someone into a cabaret rather than out."

When I returned to Adelaide, Annie organised a blind date to a horror movie, which gives you permission to clutch at people sitting nearby. Roy was the person sitting next to me, and yes, we clutched and connected.

We've now been married for 47 years and together for 48. We had a son together, and sometime after our wedding, my children from my first marriage were returned to me after a heart-rending few years' absence.

Roy has been a stalwart supporter and actively encouraged my various studies over the years, including my PhD in Communications. We live in Adelaide and have done so since the children entered high school.

That car crash led to a whole new life, love and career. It truly was so unexpected. A blessing with impact indeed!

The precious gift of life

A thank you letter from a transplant recipient to their organ donor

Thank you with all of my heart, mind, body and soul for donating your kidney and pancreas to me.

You've given me the precious gift of life, and there are no words to express my gratitude, nor my sorrow that you had to lose your life in order to give me mine.

I'll think of you every day, thank you every day, shed tears for you every day, and pray for your family and friends every day.

You've done for me what no one else has or could, and 'thank you' seems such a small phrase for such a monumental thing.

We're forever bonded in life and death. You're in me, and I'm in you.

I hold a space in my heart for you, where you'll live forever and have the life that you should have lived. This way, I'm able to do for you what you've done for me: give you life.

I love you. Thank you.

I don't want to die! I'm 21 years old, and I want to be a chef!

by Erick Jimenez

Guadalajara | Jalisco | Mexico

Hello, my name is Erick. I'm from Guadalajara in Mexico, and this is my story.

All my life, I wanted to be a chef because I like cooking, but something happened one day that I didn't expect. I got a black pimple on the lower part of my back. At the time, I didn't worry, and I was busy studying at university.

A few weeks passed, and I felt a lot of pain in my back. I noticed that the pimple had got bigger, so I decided to go to the doctor. He ordered some tests, and when the results came back, the doctor looked me in the face and told me, "Erick, you have skin cancer. It's a very aggressive melanoma."

At that moment, I felt like I was dying. I was terrified and asked the doctor if I was going to die.

The doctor said, "No, Erick, we're going to operate on you to remove that melanoma."

The day of the operation arrived, and the doctor told me that my melanoma was very large and spreading throughout my lymphatic system. I had surgery and was sent for chemotherapy, but after several months, something appeared under my armpit. It was a large tumour, weighing three kilos.

I had another operation, but I was exhausted by now and didn't have the strength to continue. I was screaming inside: *I don't want to die! I'm 21 years old, and I want to be a chef!*

I started crying and asked God to help me by sending me a divine cure to cleanse me with his precious blood.

Divine intervention

I've always had a lot of faith in God, and I believe in miracles. I want to tell you how I recovered.

I was sitting in my wheelchair. The chemotherapy and radiotherapy were consuming me. They helped stop the cancer, but they weakened me a lot.

Then, a message came from my father, and he told me, "Erick, there's a doctor who's discovered how to destroy melanoma cancers." He told me that, in Mexico, they were already treating patients.

At that moment, I felt hope. I felt that God had heard me, and I started to cry with joy. I simply said, "Thank you, God, for listening to me."

Healing

I had cancer in my chest, lungs, brain and my entire lymphatic system. I thought I was going to die. I couldn't walk; I was in a wheelchair. I had horrible pains all over my body and had to take morphine.

I started immunotherapy treatment with the new medicine, and I asked God to help me. Then, a miracle came into my life.

I remember that my father and all my brothers were with me, talking and giving me encouragement. Suddenly, I felt something in my body. I felt something begin to fall off. I immediately took the bandages off my chest and everyone could see how the pieces were beginning to fall off my chest.

We all started to cry with joy. We all said, "Thank you, God; thank you, God."

Today, I'm 31 years old and I'm completely cured. I regularly have a positron emission tomography (PET) scan, which is a type of tomography that uses a blue liquid to identify if there are any abnormal cells in my body. So far, the results have been negative.

Today, I work as a chef and my dream has come true, but my life is different. It's better. The experience of nearly losing my life has opened my eyes and given me a new perspective. I appreciate life much more than I did previously, and I'm much more mature.

I feel that God helped me and gave me another chance at life, so now I help others who are less fortunate than me. I give my time freely and cook for various charities associated with my local church.

Never lose faith in God and in yourself. The Divine is something very powerful that we all have inside us, and trusting in it is called faith.

If I hadn't been bullied, I wouldn't be running a successful business from home now

Just me...

I'm glad you're still here. It's been busy, with everyone coming and going, hasn't it? I love hearing people's stories, though. I learn so much, and I've always said everyone has a book inside them.

Here's a story that concluded brilliantly – in the end!

I worked somewhere once where I was very happy. I loved the job, I was very fulfilled and I loved the people I worked with. People make a place, don't they?

Then, my boss left. He was replaced by someone completely different. That's not necessarily a bad thing, but this person was a bully, which was a terrible thing. My new boss bullied a lot of people, including me. They undermined me, set me up to fail and constantly questioned my ability. This person even tried to frame me for something I didn't do.

One by one, people started leaving.

I stuck it out for a while, but it became apparent that nothing was going to change, and nothing I did or said made a difference. The bullying was making me sick. I felt so stressed. I was so traumatised. I couldn't sleep. I didn't know how to stop it, and I couldn't see a way out.

So, I started thinking about my options. I wanted to work from home and be my own boss. For a long time, I researched different jobs I could do. But nothing felt right, and all enquiries led to a dead end.

Then, one day, I bumped into someone I knew in town, and they told me what they were doing. A light bulb switched on in my head.

That's it! I thought, *It's obvious, and I get to use my existing skills.*

When I got home, I did a Google search. I made a phone call and spent an hour talking to someone. I subsequently enrolled on a course, studied in my free time and, several months later, emerged with a diploma.

In my spare time – and there wasn't much of that – I touted for work, built a website, printed business cards and generally promoted my fledgling business in as many ways as possible.

One day, someone took a punt on me. Hallelujah! After that, jobs slowly started rolling in, and I fitted them in on my days off. It took a long time to earn people's respect, but I was getting there – one step at a time.

Eventually, I established enough of a client base to allow me to quit my job.

It was hard work, and for the first time ever, I didn't have a guaranteed income – but I was happy and making my own decisions.

Now, I run a successful business from home, and I couldn't be happier. I don't even need to advertise or promote my work, as I get so much repeat business and so many referrals.

I never thought I would, but I silently thank my bullying former boss from time to time, because if it weren't for them, I wouldn't be where I am now.

What a blessing their bullying turned out to be.

Grazie mille. (A thousand thanks.)

Blessing bites

- When somebody bullies and undermines you, it's probably because they're unhappy, stressed or traumatised in some way.
- A bully is likely reacting to negative things happening in their own life, but they're responding to it in an unhealthy way.
- Whatever is going on in a bully's life doesn't excuse their behaviour, but it might help you understand it.
- Bullying isn't about you. It's about the bully, the way they feel and how they choose to express themselves.
- Don't ever blame yourself. When someone bullies you, it's not your fault.
- Don't tolerate bullying behaviour. Speak to someone about it and get help if you feel you need to.
- You can sometimes turn bullying to your advantage and use it to make a positive change to your life.
- Being bullied can be a springboard for something new or for taking inspired action.
- Your happiness and sense of well-being are more important than anything.

The idea had formed in my mind that I wouldn't live to see the next summer

by Teresa Misser

Rome | Italy

More than two years have passed since the life-changing events I'm about to share with you. I finally have the serenity to tell you something about my recent life that I previously didn't dare to talk about or even think about. As they say, after some time has passed, things are seen from a different perspective, as if we can view them more calmly, peacefully and objectively.

In October 2019, during a routine check-up, doctors discovered I had breast cancer. The news devastated me. I was terrified – especially so because my situation seemed to be serious. Also, I didn't think I could face the therapies that were necessary to treat me, because I'd need to take them for a long time and they'd be very heavy going.

I was fortunate that I had good doctors and clinical staff around me who encouraged me with their words and attitude. I thank heaven for this. But most and best of all, I had my family. My husband and our three boys huddled around me and never let me out of their sight. They didn't leave my side. They've been my greatest blessing.

To help you understand my state of mind when I received the news of my illness, I'll tell you this story.

In October, it starts to get cold here in Rome. The leaves on the trees along the Tiber River and also near *mia casa* (my home) in the Castelli Romani turn yellow, red and brown. At this time of year, I usually store my summer clothes away in a closet and bring my winter clothes to where they're close at hand. In 2019, however, I gave away all my summer clothes to the Caritas charity – every single last item of summer clothing. I didn't keep anything with me, only the winter stuff. I had a total clear out. The idea had formed in my mind that I wouldn't live to see the next summer, and therefore my light and fresh summer clothes would no longer be needed.

In the two years since my diagnosis, I've spent entire days in the hospital, and I've met people – both patients and health workers – who are still in my heart now. We endured our treatments at a very difficult time – during the Covid-19 pandemic. I became close to those who were worse off than me. I feel that the time lived in these two years expanded. It has passed more slowly.

I learned to get on better with people, to be patient with my parents and my dear family, to not get angry so often, and to let go of the little misunderstandings of every day.

I also stopped clock-watching and keeping track of the time. I do fewer things each day, but I still get everything done. I take on less because no one is superman or superwoman. In addition, I have fewer possessions because, after all, we don't need them.

I keep a small number of people close to me: the important ones. These relationships are sincere. We all need others, and we can give so much, but if we try to give too much to too many, we spread ourselves too thinly.

As has happened to many people around the world, an ugly event – a seemingly insurmountable difficulty – became a blessing.

Ciò che non ti distrugge può sicuramente cambiare la tua vita in meglio. (What doesn't destroy you can definitely change your life for the better.)

Your angels were protecting you

Hello again

Don't you just love that road-trip song 'Born To Be Wild' by Steppenwolf? I do. I feel the wind in my hair, my foot on the accelerator and a huge sense of exhilaration.

I was driving to Wales one day, in my Land Rover, with Daisy Boo in the back. It's a trip I made every few weeks for many years to visit my parents. I always stopped en route so Daisy and I could both stretch our legs, go to the toilet and have some lunch.

On this particular occasion, I stopped at my favourite motorway services. It's my favourite because there's a large field at the back that's perfect for walking Daisy. When we returned to the car, I reached into my jacket pocket for the key fob and…

"Oh no! Where is it?"

It started to rain. My bag was in the car, and my phone was in my bag. The key fob was somewhere in the large field of long grass we'd just walked around.

I retraced my steps as best I could with Daisy. But 30 minutes of searching later, I still hadn't found the key fob. So, I resolved to ask someone if I could borrow their phone to call for help.

Suddenly, a few metres from the car, in some long, damp grass, I saw the unmistakeable black electronic device. My heart soared with gratitude. I nearly cried with relief.

After picking it up, I unlocked the car, popped Daisy in the back with a gravy bone, and sent a text to my sister to tell her about my close encounter with disaster.

"Your angels were protecting you," she texted back. "If you hadn't lost your key fob, you'd have driven off sooner and probably been involved in an accident."

Wow. I never looked at it like that, but hey, maybe she was right?

Whether you believe that or not doesn't matter. It's a nice way to look at a difficult or frustrating situation. It takes the sting out of unpleasant feelings.

I like to believe – I choose to believe – that I was being protected. It was a blessing to lose my key fob in the long grass because the angels were looking out for me. They were keeping me safe. Thinking that felt so much better than beating myself up for losing the fob because I didn't look after it properly.

It's also given me a story to tell you.

Le benedizioni sono ovunque. (Blessings are everywhere.)

Blessing bites

- If you lose your key fob – or anything else, for that matter – it's natural to worry, but try not to panic or get angry.
- Urging others not to over react in difficult, frightening or frustrating situations is easier said than done, I know, but try not to let your emotions overwhelm you.
- Worry is a completely useless and wasted emotion because it never causes a situation to result in a positive outcome.
- Worry depletes your energy and robs you of your peace of mind.
- Focus instead on how to solve the issue at hand.
- Take deep breaths, relax and think about how best to respond.
- Replace worry with trust that everything will be OK.
- Trust that you can and will cope with whatever has happened.
- Visualise a positive outcome, as it'll help to calm you, so you can then think more clearly about what to do.

- Be aware of how you're feeling and what you're doing.
- Accept that uncertainty is part of life, and whilst you can't control everything, you can control how you think about things.
- Whether or not you believe in angels doesn't matter. If it helps you rationalise a challenging situation, that's OK.
- You're not hurting anyone if you believe in angels – or goblins, fairies, elves, pixies, leprechauns, pink elephants, etc.

A soul braving the world

by Zerah Garrote

Dubai | United Arab Emirates

So many blessings have happened to me, but my mind always seems to find a reason to doubt how miraculous everything has been.

Then, one day, I asked God to show me a miracle and move me to a new home. It happened almost straight away. The exact image I had in my mind of the home I wanted appeared suddenly on my phone, and I knew the place was made for me.

It wasn't ready for me to move into, as it still had occupants, but the landlady asked me to wait until the following day. Later, she messaged me to say I could stay there for the night after all, as everything I needed was available, and the flat only needed cleaning in the morning.

I took the place immediately and left my old home at once. The journey there was bumpy, and my things were rolling around in the car. I forgot that I'd brought the eggs from my fridge, and I only remembered this when I transferred my things up to the flat.

I mistakenly dropped a bag, and it popped open with the carton of eggs. I thought, *Oh no! The eggs must be broken.*

But then an angel whispered in my ear, "They're safe."

When I got inside my new apartment, I opened the carton to check the eggs, and lo and behold, they were left untouched, as if they'd never gone through a rough ride and accidental dropping. It was such a blessing.

I wept because God had shown me that, no matter what turbulent waters you come through and no matter how many times you fall, you're safe and you're protected.

Whilst I was crying, I noticed the art work on the wall of my new flat. It contained the words "Fall seven times. Stand up eight times."

I thought, *I can conquer the world.*

I grew to fit the shape of my shell

Gaia: "What are you looking for?"

Claude: "My home. It's been washed away by a giant wave."

Gaia: "What does it look like?"

Claude: "It's a green turbo shell with brown splotches. Not too big and not too small. It has a large, round entrance, and it's lined with mother of pearl."

Gaia: "Sounds lovely."

Claude: "It is, and I want it back."

Gaia: "It also sounds like every other shell on the beach. Why don't you look for another one to make your home?"

Claude: "I don't want another shell. I like that one. Besides, it did a brilliant job of protecting me. It kept me safe, comfortable and dry."

Gaia: "We don't always get what we want. We don't always get to keep things the same way, no matter how much we want to."

Claude: "I grew to fit the shape of my shell. *Non capisci.* [You don't understand.]"

Gaia: "I do, actually, and I'm sorry you've lost your home.

	"I lost mine once too. Like you, I'd grown into it. But something happened, and I had to leave, though I ended up finding something better.
	"I just had to let go of my attachment first."
Claude:	"What happened?"
Gaia:	"I had a beautiful, old home in a picture-postcard village. It was perfect in every way. It had three bedrooms, three bathrooms and a wine cellar. It even had a fish pond and a fountain in the garden."
Claude:	"Sounds idyllic."
Gaia:	"It was, especially the garden. It was a memory garden – one full of plants given to me by people I love. I'd even planted a tree in memory of a family friend who died.
	"Every time I looked at a particular flower or tree, I was reminded of the person who gave it to me."
Claude:	"What a beautiful idea! So what happened?"
Gaia:	"My husband and I got divorced, and we had to sell the house."
Claude:	"That sucks."
Gaia:	"It turned out to be a blessing in disguise.
	"You see, I stayed in the marriage way longer than I should have because I didn't want to lose the house. It was the wrong reason not to move on.

"Some friends who tried to be supportive said, 'It's only bricks and mortar.'

"However, I didn't see it that way at the time. All I saw was that I'd worked so hard for – and looked after – what I had, and now I'd have to leave everything behind because of someone else's behaviour. It made me feel resentful.

"That resentment ate away at me and kept me stuck."

Claude: "But I'm in a completely different situation to you. My home has been taken from me by a wave. You chose to leave yours."

Gaia: "It doesn't matter how we lose something that's important to us. Sometimes, it serves us better to accept our situation and remember the serenity prayer."

Claude: "What's that?"

Gaia: "'Grant me the serenity to accept the things I cannot change, the courage to change the things I can and the wisdom to know the difference.'"

Claude: "I like the sound of that, but how does that apply to me?"

Gaia: "A wave has taken your home. You can't change what's happened. You can't change the past. The wave that took your home is behind you now."

Claude: "What? It's coming again?"

Gaia: "I don't mean literally.

"You can't get your home back, but you can find a new one. Maybe your new home will be better than your old one, and you'll be glad the wave came along when it did."

Claude: "Is that what happened with you?"

Gaia: "It sure was. That's why I'm telling you this story: to give you some comfort and hope.

"Not only did I have to give up my precious home and garden, but I also had to leave behind the community I'd become a part of."

Claude: "You're not selling this to me."

Gaia: "However, I moved close to my family. I hardly ever saw them before, but when I bought my new home near them, I saw them all the time.

"It was brilliant. We made new memories together."

Claude: "And your new home, what was that like?"

Gaia: "A million times better than my old one. It has everything I want and need, and more."

Claude: "Is that where you are now?"

Gaia: "Sure is.

"When I look back, things were always going wrong in the old house. The boiler was forever breaking down, even the new one! The plumbing problems were endless, and nothing seemed to fit or work properly. One side of the house, which was exposed to the wind and rain, was always damp, and the curtain rods came away from the wall because the plaster was weak.

"I can see now that the house was a reflection of the people who lived in it. Our relationship didn't work, so the house didn't work.

"My new home is light and bright, even on an overcast day. It's warm in winter and cool in summer. It's not too big and not too small. Everything works perfectly, exactly as it's meant to.

"The house works, because I work as a person."

Claude: "Maybe you were just lucky."

Gaia: "Luck has nothing to do with it. I had an unshakable belief that I'd be alright and that everything would unfold as it was meant to and would work out exactly as it was supposed to.

"I had faith. I created my future with positive thoughts, a positive attitude and positive action."

Claude: "How many bathrooms do you have?"

Gaia: "That's hardly relevant, but it has one. I can only use one bathroom at a time, so why would I want more?

"More rooms means more cleaning and more maintenance, which equals less time to spend doing the things I love."

Claude: "I guess so."

Gaia: "Come on. Let's find you a nice new shell to make your home."

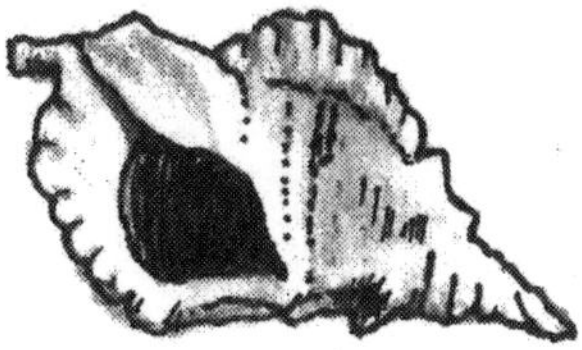

Blessing bites

- You don't always get what you want.
- You don't always get to keep things the same way, no matter how much you want to.
- Not getting what you want can turn out to be a good thing: a blessing in disguise.
- Sometimes, when bad things happen, you end up finding something better.
- To move forward, you have to let go of your attachment to the thing you're holding on to first, whether it's your home, your job, a person or something else.
- Letting go is the only way you can move forward successfully.
- You can maintain the status quo, even when things are unpleasant, but you'll stay stuck.
- Holding on when you should let go means you won't grow to reach your full potential.
- If you keep feeding your fear of the unknown, you'll miss out on so many, possibly life-changing, opportunities.
- You should find the right reasons to change things that don't work for you, rather than keeping things the same for the wrong reasons.

- It doesn't matter how we lose something that's important to us. Sometimes, it serves us better to accept our situation and remember the serenity prayer: "Grant me the serenity to accept the things I cannot change, the courage to change the things I can and the wisdom to know the difference."
- You can't change the things that have happened, no matter how much you want to.
- You can't change the past. It's behind you, and you'll never get it back.
- The beauty of having something behind you is that it forces you to focus on the present and look forward to the future.
- Looking to the future allows you to find something new, and maybe it'll be better.
- Sometimes, there's a reason why things go wrong or don't work.
- The signs are there, and you just need to see and understand them.
- Your outer world reflects your inner world.
- When things work, it's usually because you work as a person (i.e. you're functioning well).

- Try to cultivate an unshakable belief that everything will be alright. You'll feel more calm and peaceful.
- Everything will unfold as it's meant to and will work out exactly as it's supposed to.
- Have faith, and create your future with positive thoughts, a positive attitude and positive action.
- You're the only person in the world who can do this. No one can do it for you. See how powerful you are!

How a nasty accident gave me valuable time to help look after my new granddaughter

by Cilla Peck

Walmer | Kent | England

As I drove the 20-mile journey to work, with mixed amounts of traffic, it was a typically autumnal morning: cold and damp, but with beautiful sunshine and a blue sky.

I arrived in the city and parked my van in the road just behind the office in good time to take a walk before I started my working day.

I won't deny that my mind was still full of joy and excitement at the arrival of my granddaughter, Penny, a few days before. It was also full of my deep relief that my daughter was home safely and recovering well, despite the usual trials, tribulations and concerns of being a new parent with a precious little bundle to care for and love.

As I walked to the edge of the pavement, deciding whether to go right or left, the next thing I knew I was flying through the air and landed heavily on my right wrist. As I scrambled to my feet to make my way to the office door – the keys already in my hand – I peeked at the damage as I held my arm. It was fairly obvious that I'd dislocated the wrist joint. I discovered later that I'd also fractured the end of my radius.

Oh boy, that was bad timing! Yep, I'm right-handed, and all my nanna duties flew through my head in a whirl of panic, guilt and disappointment. How on earth had this happened? Well, I think the edge of my shoe caught a raised, mossy or damp kerbstone, and the rest, as they say, is history.

I'll spare you the rather boring and traumatic events of my trip to the local hospital's minor injuries department, and the subsequent surgery the following day to plate and pin my wrist into place, but suffice to say that it was an experience I'd rather not have had.

What I haven't told you so far is that I live alone. My daughter Hannah and son-in-law Nick had recently moved to the small town where I live, which is a semi-rural place on the south-east coast of England.

My daughter is very precious to me, because 33 years ago, my husband died suddenly when I was four months pregnant, so you could say there's another blessing already in place (the blessing of my fractured wrist is yet to be revealed!), as Hannah gave me a reason to live after my husband's death.

Back to the present day. Thankfully, Hannah and Nick asked me to stay with them for the first week after my accident and surgery. So, I started my new vocation of being a nanna, whilst learning to use my left hand for everything, including the all-important cuddles, and making tea and biscuits to sustain a very tired new mum – my daughter.

And here's where the blessing comes in. Because I slipped and broke my wrist, I had time off work to recover, which meant I was available to help my daughter and son-in-law navigate the early days of parenthood and to help care for Penny so they could sleep.

It's fair to say that they, in turn, looked after me.

I have a fiercely independent streak, which meant I wasn't a good patient.

However, with much understanding and love from my lovely little family, not to mention a few very good friends, I had the privilege of being able to see, help and support Hannah, Nick and Penny through the precious – and sometimes very challenging – early days and nights of Penny's first few days and weeks in this amazing world.

As I couldn't drive, my wonderful friends – one of whom is the author of this book – ferried me about so I could let the new little family have some precious time alone together to make and seal their first memories.

Naturally, there were ups and downs, and smiles, laughter and tears, but I've now recovered fully and I'm able to look back on that time with a sense of gratitude.

There have been many other trials and tribulations over the past few years. We've lived through a pandemic affecting the whole world, and – like others – have suffered loss and sadness.

But today, I gaze out of the window at a bright-blue sky, with a bowl of daffodils on the table and an abundance of love in my heart. It'll soon be spring, and despite all that's happening around the world, I'll continue to look forward and gaze up into the beautiful universe, taking care not to let my foot slip on a mossy kerbstone!

This story is dedicated to my beautiful daughter, Hannah; my granddaughter, Penny; my son-in-law, Nick; and some amazing friends. You know who you are. Thank you, I love you all so much.

Blessings come in many shapes and sizes

A blessing is a feeling. An emotion. Energy in motion.
It's being held in the heart of hope fulfilled.

A blessing is finding the 'can' in 'can't', the 'do' in 'don't', the 'ease' in 'disease', the 'order' in 'disorder', and the 'possible' in 'impossible'.

A blessing is Mother Earth doing her best.

A blessing is forgiving yourself for giving yourself away.

A blessing is shedding your metaphorical skin, so you can grow.

A blessing is meeting someone in a field one day and that chance meeting becoming a catalyst for positive transformation.

A blessing is reaching out in the darkness and a stranger taking your hand and showing you the way home.

A blessing is meditating in nature.

A blessing is when you silently ask the Universe for the little robin to sit on your shoulder, and he does.

A blessing is when a person whom you thought would always be there for you doesn't show up, because they just made space in your life for someone who's better for your well-being.

A blessing is when a friend sends you a photo of Saint Mary MacKillop because it's said to bring blessings, and your friend knows you need them.

A blessing is falling asleep to the sound of your dog breathing softly, and then waking up to the sound of your dog breathing softly.

A blessing is when something good comes from something bad.

A blessing is living your dreams twice: in your imagination first, and then when they come true.

A blessing is when a friend who lives half a world away sends you a daisy from her garden because she knows you love them.

Healthy boundaries are a blessing – a massive blessing. They keep you safe and grounded.

A blessing is when the light at the end of the tunnel is behind you.

Le benedizioni sono molto belle. (The blessings are very beautiful.)

With so much pain in my heart, I started screaming at God

by Carmen Jimenez

Guadalajara | Jalisco | Mexico

Hello, my name is Carmen Jimenez. I live in Jalisco, Mexico, and this is my sad but fascinating story.

Since I was a little girl, I've always dreamed of marrying the perfect man. With this man of my dreams, I'd have children and create a beautiful family full of love.

In my youth, I had many boyfriends, but none were perfect – until Juan came along. I was 14 years old and the happiest person on earth because Juan was very handsome, hard-working and funny.

When I turned 16, Juan asked me to marry him. I couldn't believe it; I was going to marry the man of my dreams!

The change

I was married to Juan for 10 years. We had three children and a restaurant that earned us a good living, and we were so very happy.

Then, everything started to change. My Juan began drinking with his friends, and for several days, he didn't come home to sleep. I was told that he gambled a lot of money on cards and went around with other women.

I started to cry, and I said to myself, "What's going on? Why has my Juan changed? Why does he play cards, billiards and dice, and bet with the money we worked so hard for in the restaurant? And why does he have other women?"

To cut a long story short, my hell lasted for more than 15 years. My old Juan had gone.

During that time, my parents and brothers told me to leave that trash of a man. They said I should dedicate myself to my children and myself, and that I could manage the restaurant alone.

God

One day, I was sitting at the table and, with so much pain in my heart, I started screaming at God: "*Lord, why is this happening to me? If you gave me my Juan, why don't you help me to get him back?*"

I cried every day, asking God for an answer, but nothing happened.

It was like that for many days, but despite everything, I still had a lot of faith in God, and I asked him every day to bring my husband back to me.

The miracle

Several years later, I was feeding my children one day, and the front door opened. My husband came in drunk and very distressed.

He said to me, "Carmen, my love, forgive me. Here I am. I realise all the damage I've caused you. I realise all the mistakes I've made.

"I want to change. If you forgive me, I promise I'll never drink again. I'll never play cards or gamble again.

"Today, I almost got killed because I had no money to pay for a bet, and I said to God, 'Lord, if you help me out of this problem, I promise to stop gambling and go back to my wife and my children.'

"So here I am. Forgive me, my wife; forgive me."

The outcome

God performed a miracle, and my Juan underwent an incredible change. We've been married for more than 30 years now. He left all his vices behind and is totally dedicated to me and our family.

I want to tell you that I've achieved my dream. I now have my perfect husband, my three children and my 10 grandchildren. We're all together, happy, and full of much love and many blessings.

I even found some blessings living with an alcoholic

Ciao di nuovo! (Hello again!)

If you knew me, you'd never have guessed that I had a dirty little secret.

I'm a strong, confident, independent career woman who has worked with some very high-profile people in two countries. I've travelled the world, I've been on an expedition, I'm self-reliant and I've lived in different parts of the globe.

I'm not at all the kind of person you'd think lived with an addict, but I did. An alcoholic. An angry person who got angrier with beer in his belly – so there was domestic abuse as well. This wasn't physical violence; it was verbal violence – emotional and psychological abuse.

I could write a book about the decade and more of trauma I suffered, but this is about blessings, and guess what? I even found some blessings whilst living with an alcoholic. So, fasten your seatbelt because you might be interested in this bit, given that alcohol abuse is so prevalent around the world.

I'll refer to the alcoholic as 'the lodger', because most of the time he only came home to eat and sleep. The rest of the time the lodger was indulging his addiction elsewhere.

Let's get back to the blessings, because I want to give comfort to others who find themselves living with, or adversely affected by, an addict.

It doesn't matter what that person is addicted to - drugs, alcohol, gambling, food or sex - their behaviour has a huge negative impact on the people they live with. They tend to blame others for their addiction, and they don't have any remorse for their behaviour or the consequences of it.

The lodger was heavily addicted to gambling too, by the way.

Anyway, I'll go back to the blessings, because there were so many of them, and I'm grateful for each and every one.

During my dark nights of the soul, before I found the courage to leave, I tried helping myself in many varied ways. One way was to count all the wonderful blessings I had as a direct result of the lodger being in my life.

Now, that was a big ask, but if I can do it, so can you. There will be things you're so thankful for because of your addict. You might have to dig deep, but give it a go.

Here are my blessings that arose because of the lodger:

1. My favourite painting was brought to magical life. Since I was eight years old, I've been obsessed with Salvador Dali. The painting I love best and the one that got me hooked on the surrealist artist is *The Persistence of Memory.*

   The lodger bought tickets for us to visit Dali's house in Port Lligat, Spain - which is now a museum - and I got to see the view in my favourite painting in real life.

The lodger brought that to life for me, and I'll never ever forget it.

2. I have a dog who is my funny, faithful, ever-present companion. I wouldn't be without her. She's the most precious thing in my life. The lodger gave me the dog as a gift, and I have to say that she's the best present I've ever received. I credit her with saving my life.

   She filled the space the lodger left. She's brilliant company. She comes with me to visit my family and friends. She gets me out and about exercising. She gives me purpose and gives my life meaning. She costs me an absolute fortune, but I don't have any other vices, so I don't care. It's only money.

   I'll always be grateful to the lodger for giving me the greatest gift of all: my dog.

3. I moved to an area that I never would have otherwise because the lodger wanted to live there. It's beautiful. It's not as picturesque as what I left behind in our previous home together, but I'm near the sea, I'm surrounded by woods and fields, and I live in a lovely old house full of character and history.

   There's a huge garden that comes with it, where I can lose myself in nature and my dog can play. I'm so very blessed.

4. I have friends whom I never would have met had I not moved here. Some of these people will be friends for life – I know it. We have much in common, and they're great fun and a massive support.

5. I do yoga, which is great for my body and mind. I wanted to meet new people and make friends when I moved to this area, and the lodger found a leaflet in our local fish and chip shop. The lodger brought it home, I made a phone call, and the next minute, I was enrolled in my first yoga class. My yoga teacher is now one of my closest friends, so how's that for a blessing?

6. I've become an integral part of both my local dog and village communities. I've made wonderful friends here, we give and receive support to/from each other, and they kept me sane when my world was falling apart.

7. I run my own business. The lodger and I were shopping in town one day when we bumped into a former colleague of his. A conversation with this person led to me quitting my job, training, establishing and, subsequently, running a very successful business from home.

   Thank you, lodger. Because of you, I was in a town I wouldn't have been shopping in. I met one of your former colleagues, whom I wouldn't have known if it wasn't for you. We had a conversation that we wouldn't have had, and I'm now doing something I love that I probably wouldn't have thought of.

8. I found spiritualism, which – along with my dog – helped save my life. I was looking for something to help me cope with the lodger's behaviour, and I found spirituality – or it found me. I don't know which way around it was, but we found each other and we're very happy together, thank you.

   As I became more spiritual, I realised I'd been repeating negative patterns of behaviour that contributed to me forming intimate relationships with the wrong people. People with bad energy were attracted to me, and they sucked the good energy out of me.

   I was a people-pleaser. I was too willing to fit in, make do, put up with, sacrifice and do without so people like the lodger could get their own way and feel better about themselves.

   I, wrongly, made other people responsible for my happiness: *big mistake!* I, and I alone, am responsible for my happiness.

   I made myself small and dimmed my light so the lodger could feel more important and in control. I knew something was wrong; my gut was screaming at me, but I ignored my intuition. This was another big mistake, because my gut was telling me that if I have to change my behaviour to fit in with someone else, something is very wrong.

I now have healthy boundaries and, consequently, attract stable, well-adjusted people whom I'm aligned with in every way. All future relationships, no matter what form they take, will be so much more rewarding because healthy people attract other healthy people.

Broken and needy people attract other broken and needy people. I must have been needy to do myself the great disservice of changing who I was so the lodger could feel special.

Spirituality is in my tool kit now for dealing with all situations and circumstances that arise – both good and bad. It should be in your tool kit too.

So, I say a massive thank you to the lodger, because without him, I may never have found spirituality, and I wouldn't be without it now.

9. I know exactly what I do and don't want, and what I will and won't put up with. The lodger has been a great teacher – or rather, the lessons I've learned are a blessed consequence of the lodger's behaviour.

   I thank the lodger silently every day for all the blessings he's brought into my life. I choose to see the good that came out of our union, rather than the toxic consequences of his alcoholism and gambling. I concentrate on the blessings and the countless wonderful opportunities that have presented themselves as a result, and all the things I have that I wouldn't have otherwise.

There's a saying that good overcomes evil. Well, finding the blessings in a relationship with an addict is a perfect example of that, and it's so much better than focusing on the harm the addict causes. It's empowering. It gives you back some of the control you give away, or feel you've lost, when you're constantly making allowances for someone else's addiction.

Blessing bites

- If you can find the blessings in living with, or knowing, an addict, you can find them virtually anywhere.
- Finding the blessings might provide some comfort to those who find themselves living with, or adversely affected by, an addict's behaviour.
- When you start counting your blessings, and do so in the hardest of places, you'll realise there were more than you thought, and you'll be thankful for each and every one.
- When you live with an addict, you have to find ways to help yourself cope with their negative behaviour.
- One way to cope with another's negative behaviour is to count all the wonderful blessings as a direct or indirect result of having them in your life.
- You might have to dig deep, but give it a go. There are likely to be some hidden blessings.
- Your addict has probably done something nice for you or given you something special, or their behaviour may have inadvertently led to you finding something wonderful that you no longer want to live without. What are those things?

- ☼ Addiction can be a great teacher to those of us who live, or have lived, with an addict.
- ☼ It helps you understand exactly what you do and don't want, and what you will and won't tolerate.
- ☼ Thank your addict silently every day for all the blessings they've brought into your life.
- ☼ Choose to see the good that comes, or came, out of you knowing your addict, rather than the toxic consequences of their addiction.
- ☼ Remind yourself of the countless wonderful opportunities that may have presented themselves as a direct or indirect result of your addict.
- ☼ Finding the blessings in a relationship with an addict is so much better than focusing on the harm the addict causes.
- ☼ If you're feeling generous, you can also intellectualise the fact that your addict is probably nursing a lot of pain, self-loathing, low self-esteem and, likely, a mental health problem, so they deserve your compassion.

B stands for blessings

Hello friend ♡

This is my personal **A** to **Z** of blessings:

Animals, **a**rt and **A**ustralia

Blessings

Colour, **c**hocolate, **c**louds and **c**offee

Dogs, **d**ogs, **d**ogs – *I love dogs*

Energy

Family and **f**riends

Good health, **g**ratitude and *gelato* (ice cream)

Home and **h**igh vibration

Italy and **i**magination

Just be

Kindle the love and light within

Law of attraction, **l**essons and **l**ove

Music, **m**ountains, **m**editation, **M**exico, **m**agic and **m**ellifluous (such a beautiful word!)

Nature

Oh how wonderful!

Positive thoughts and emotions

Quantum physics

Rainbows and **r**aindrops

Sunshine, **s**piritual awakening, **S**alvador Dali and **s**oul family

Trees and **t**ravel

Understanding, **u**nicorns and the **UK**

Vieni con me (come with me)

Waterfalls, **w**armth and **w**atermelons

X-ray vision

Yoga

Zesty, **z**any and **z**en

What's your A to Z of blessings?

Now it's your turn. Take a break from reading, grab a notebook, pen or pencil, and write down your blessings. Hidden or not so hidden – it's up to you.

What are the things that ameliorate (such a blessedly beautiful word) your soul?

Once you start, it's hard to stop, as the blessings just keep rolling in like waves onto a seashore.

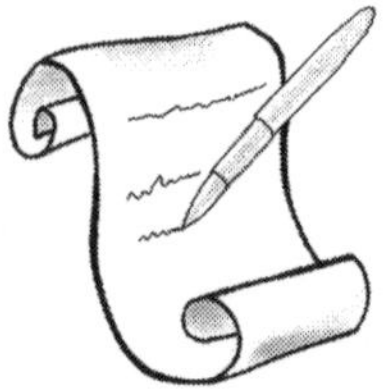

The gift of a dog that changed our lives forever

by Amanda Lynch

Canberra | Australian Capital Territory | Australia

Some people say you can't buy love. That's true, but it is the case that you can choose love, and this story is about the gift of a dog that changed our lives forever.

Gerard, a toy poodle, was a squirming bundle of black curls, limbs and a tongue like an anteater when he arrived at my place and was extricated from the lap of my niece, Zoe. She'd held him during the car trip from the farm in Goulburn, New South Wales, where he came from.

Everything about dog–human friendship was new to me: mealtimes, walks, playtime and long periods of rest.

It was a time when my whole world had been turned upside down by a diagnosis of breast cancer. At the outset, a puppy seemed to me to be yet another responsibility that I didn't have time for. But contrary to initial expectations, he turned out to be a ray of light at a very difficult time.

The doctor had said that regular exercise was important during the chemotherapy and radiotherapy treatment, despite me having low energy levels.

Little Gerard soon got used to routines and would demand a walk twice a day. To have responsibility for another little soul certainly curtailed any feelings of self-pity. When I was so tired that I just wanted a nap, I'd wake to find him on the couch next to me, doing the same thing, often with his favourite toy tiger as well.

Of course, there was puppy training involved, and my sister Sara and niece helped with that. Their poodle, Louis, was Gerard's cousin, and he taught Gerard how to dig up bones and where and how to cock a leg.

It's 12 years later, and I still have little Gerard, who is such a special part of my life. But now there are three of us, and Gerard was there to witness another blessing.

I met my future husband on a picnic at the Botanic Gardens, and Colin and Gerard hit it off immediately. When he came to visit me, Colin would bring over presents for Gerard: a pig's ear one time, and a blanket or a toy monkey the next. When we had sleepovers at Colin's apartment, Gerard would always be fed the best steak from the butcher for dinner.

As I write this, we three have just returned from a caravanning trip down the Australian south coast, and we can't imagine life without each other.

Gerard has such a positive attitude, treating each day as an adventure. He also expects to be loved, sticks up for himself and has healthy self-respect. If we're late for his afternoon walk, we soon know about it, and if his dinner isn't on time, there will be not-so-gentle hints being made.

In return, he loves with a wholeheartedness, and he trusts without question the strength of the bonds that have grown so strong over the years. These are great qualities to live by and so essential for happiness.

It was a dark time when little Gerard came to me as a precious gift. Accepting this gift, which I wouldn't have received had I not been diagnosed with cancer, has provided healing, love and untold blessings, which overflow into all my relationships at work and at home.

It's better to try and fail than fail to try

Gaia:	"Have you lost something?"
Bodhi:	"My bus ticket. It must have fallen out of my pocket."
Gaia:	"Oh. I'll help you look for it, if you like?"
Bodhi:	"I wouldn't need a ticket for the bus if I hadn't failed my driving test."
Gaia:	"Sorry to hear that, but you didn't fail, you just didn't pass this time."
Bodhi:	"Is that upside-down talk designed to make me feel better?"
Gaia:	"It's better to try and fail than fail to try, and it's up to you how you want to feel. It's your choice."
Bodhi:	"I don't have a choice. I failed my test, and I feel bad about it. My parents bought me a car in advance as a present for getting my licence, and I didn't pass. "I feel like I've let them down and let myself down."
Gaia:	"That was kind of them, but you haven't let anyone down. I'm sure they don't see it that way. "Besides, the car isn't going anywhere. It'll still be there when you do pass.

"You do have a choice, by the way. You can sit there feeling sorry for yourself or you can pick yourself up, practise your driving and work on the things that caused you not to pass."

Bodhi: "Easy for you to say."

Gaia: "It is, actually. It took me three goes before I passed my driving test."

Bodhi: "And how did you feel when you failed?"

Gaia: "Upset, frustrated and angry, but I also decided to celebrate the fact that I'd taken the test in the first place. That's an achievement in itself. So when I passed, I'd celebrated three times."

Bodhi: "That's a bit weird. What did you do?"

Gaia: "I just treated myself to something I wanted at the time. It was a way of being kind to myself. I didn't want to wallow in bad feelings, so I did something that made me feel good."

Bodhi: "Sounds a bit airy-fairy. What do you think I should do then?"

Gaia: "You could try being more open-minded, for starters. I take it you're going to have another crack at trying to pass your driving test?"

Bodhi: "That goes without saying."

Gaia: "Then you've already learned something without thinking too hard about it. You've learned about perseverance, and that will stand you in good stead in other aspects of your life too."

Bodhi: "*Tipo cosa?* [Like what?]"

Gaia: "Work, for instance. Say you want a pay rise, and you don't get it. Are you going to give up at the first hurdle? Of course not. You'll find out what you need to do to convince your boss that you deserve more money, and then you'll try again. You'll keep going until you get what you want."

Bodhi: "I see what you're getting at."

Gaia: "Don't give up. You'll need a driving licence for work. It's also a valuable form of ID, and being able to drive a car gives you independence and freedom."

Bodhi: "OK, don't rub it in."

Gaia: "When we face tough times in life, giving up feels like the easiest thing to do sometimes, but there's no reward in giving up. The reward is in overcoming obstacles and succeeding at your task. Don't worry about failing; that's just a part of the process."

Bodhi: "I know. And the thought of catching a bus for the rest of my life means it just isn't an option."

Gaia: "No, it's not, and besides, there's a school of thought that says failing your driving test makes you a better driver."

Bodhi: "I'm not sure I agree with that."

Gaia: "Look at it this way: when you take your test again, you'll know exactly what to expect, so you're already at an advantage. It should make you more relaxed too."

Bodhi: "Yeah. It shouldn't be so nerve-wracking the second time around."

Gaia: "Do you know where you went wrong this time?"

Bodhi: "Sure do. It was a stupid mistake. I've driven around roundabouts dozens of times before, but this time I did it all wrong."

Gaia: "Well, maybe you just have to focus more. At least you know where you went wrong, so preparing for your next test should be easy-peasy.

"Try to get into the right frame of mind. It's not the end of the world."

Bodhi: "It just feels like it."

Gaia: "Haven't you heard a thing I've said?"

Bodhi: "What doesn't kill you makes you stronger."

Gaia: "That's more like it, and you can be sure that, when you do pass, it won't be a fluke. You'll have really earned it."

Bodhi: "You sound like my parents. They said things don't always go the way you want in life, and I should accept what's happened, learn from it and move on. It builds character, they say."

Gaia: "They sound like very smart people.

"By the way, I'm just checking, but you didn't put your bus ticket in your mobile phone case did you?"

Bodhi: "Oops. Yes, I did. Thank goodness for that. How did you know?"

Gaia: "Just a hunch."

Bodhi: "Thanks for that, and thanks for the chat. I'm going to get home and see if Dad can take me out for a drive after work."

Gaia: "Good for you, and *bocca al lupo* [good luck]."

Blessing bites

- You didn't fail, you just didn't pass this time.
- It's better to try and fail than fail to try.
- It's up to you how you want to feel. It's your choice.
- You can sit there feeling sorry for yourself, or you can pick yourself up, practise your driving (or whatever else you need to practise), and work on the things that caused you not to pass or get what you want.
- Make a conscious decision to celebrate when you don't pass or get what you want. Flip it, and celebrate the fact that you tried and gave it your best shot. That's an achievement in itself.
- Treat yourself to something you want, and be kind to yourself. You deserve it.
- Do something that makes you feel good, and stop beating yourself up.
- Persevere, and that will stand you in good stead, not just in relation to what you're aiming for now but also in other areas of your life.
- Don't give up at the first hurdle. Keep going until you get what you want.
- There's no reward in giving up. The reward is in overcoming obstacles and succeeding at your task.

- Not getting what you want the first time can just be a part of the process.
- If you have to work harder to get what you want, you know you've really and truly earned it when you get it.
- When you know where you went wrong, you've learned a valuable lesson, so you can better prepare for next time.
- Try to get into the right frame of mind.
- It isn't the end of the world if things don't work out the way you want or expect.
- What doesn't kill you makes you stronger.
- When something you want takes a different direction, try to accept it, learn from it and move on. It builds character.

A chance meeting altered the course of my life for the better

by Nigel Simpson

Perth | Western Australia | Australia

A series of extremely difficult personal challenges, which were anything but a blessing at the time, led to a chance meeting that altered the course of my life for the better.

In 2009, I joined a mental health support group after suffering from severe anxiety and depression when my dad was diagnosed with cancer. This is where I met a lady who used to live around the corner from me, and she changed my life when she joined the group too.

She encouraged me to develop my spiritual gifts and gave me the tools to develop them. She also urged me to take on a leadership role within the group, which I'd never been given the opportunity to do before.

I took on the role, which gave me more confidence, and when I left the group seven years later, I knew that I wouldn't return, and I was going to be stepping further and further out of my comfort zone.

A few weeks after leaving the group, I was talking with a lady in a crystal shop, and she showed me some crystals I'd never seen before. They were manifestation quartz. As I tried to say the word 'manifestation', I lost my voice, but I connected with the crystal so strongly that I ended up buying it.

The next day, I was looking at the crystal shop's Facebook page and I noticed an advert for a seven-week tarot card course, which was being held on a Tuesday night. Even though I didn't know much about tarot, I trusted that the Universe or God – whatever you want to call it – was guiding me. So the next day, I signed up and met with the lady who was teaching the course.

Later that same year, my parents had to go through the family court. The magistrate was known for taking a long time to make decisions, so I prayed to Archangel Michael, and the magistrate made his decision on the day of the hearing. We were grateful that he did, because a few weeks later, my dad passed away.

Several weeks after losing my dad, I met with a support worker and told her I wanted to get my learner's permit, despite having severe anxiety travelling in cars and buses. After three months of driving lessons and doing the theory exam, I was ready for my driving test. I got 30 out of 30 and received my learner's permit.

This success gave me a huge boost and led to my next manifestation.

The only fear that I hadn't conquered was my fear of flying. In July 2018, I boarded a plane and flew across Australia from Perth to Melbourne. When I reached my destination, I thoroughly enjoyed myself, walking through Australia's second biggest city and going to a football game with more than 88,000 spectators. I enjoyed my trip so much that I returned a year later.

I often think about the events that led me to where I am today. I couldn't have foreseen at the time that adversity, pain and suffering would be pivotal in turning my life around.

Bless your heart

Hi ♡

There's a very good reason for using the phrase 'bless your heart' in the true sense of wishing good things to happen to the person whose heart you're blessing.

I like to say, "Bless your beautiful heart," because it imparts much more feeling. It's a thank you with meaning. Gratitude with tangible sincerity. Sympathy and empathy in abundance.

It says, "I'll wrap you up in my big, warm, comforting words like a blanket."

It says, "I understand you. I hear you. I admire you. I respect you. I value what you've said or done."

'Bless your heart' is only three little words, but they mean so much. They pack a mighty punch.

And in an even more literal sense, you should bless your heart every day. Say thank you to it for pumping blood around your body, sending oxygen to every cell and keeping you alive.

Thank it for making between 60 and 100 beats per minute. That's between 3,600 and 6,000 beats every hour, equating to between 86,400 and 144,000 beats each day. So every week, that's between 604,800 and 1,008,000 beats in total. See how hard your heart works! If you want to work out how many beats that is per month, year and decade, please do and let me know.

Your heart is a blessing, and all this beating goes on beneath your ribcage without you having to do a thing other than just show up.

You also feel emotions in your heart. You know when that is because it beats faster than usual; maybe it feels like it's skipping a beat or it might burst; or it tickles, aches or flutters.

Your heart is a storyteller. It reacts to what's going on in your mind and tells you tales in the form of feelings. So, bless your beautiful heart for letting you know how it feels. That's important because emotions help you decide what action to take in certain situations.

Oh, and your heart – *il tuo cuore* – is a symbol of love, and love is the ultimate positive energy; when you have that, you're perfectly aligned with your intentions and your true self. Love is what you are and what you're made of.

Blessings poem

by Alan Brett

Blessings never reveal themselves;
they're always in disguise.
But subtly, you are made aware,
and then you realise.

That what's gone on before,
just by serendipity,
or maybe preordained,
in truth, show duplicity.

Something far superior,
they'll bring to you a change
that's well beyond your dreams,
your life to rearrange.

Maybe ordained by destiny,
the hidden hand of fate,
if you thought you'd met
your truly perfect mate.

Who cruelly lets you down,
your pain will not abate.
Then another brings true love
and blessings, not too late.

Or if you see your dream home
and your offer is rejected,
you'll find another better still
and get more than expected.

That is life, believe you me,
adversity in its guise.
But out of that can come
your blessings in disguise.

I don't have any money to buy food, and I'm hungry

Gaia: "Hey! What are you doing? Scram!"

Sally: "I'm having my lunch."

Gaia: "You're having someone else's!"

Sally: "They won't miss a chip or two."

Gaia: "That's not the point. It's stealing. Why do you seagulls always steal people's food?"

Sally: "I don't know about any bird else, but I don't have money to buy food, and I'm hungry."

Gaia: "*Cosa è successo?* [What happened?]"

Sally: "I had a great job, showing the fishermen where the mackerel were. My friends and I would circle above the sea and float on the water to feed sometimes, so the fishing boats knew where to cast their nets."

Gaia: "But?"

Sally: "But new fishing quotas were introduced, so the fishermen don't go out as often, which means I can't earn a living."

Gaia: "I'm sorry. Is there something else you can do?"

Sally: "I don't know. Like what?"

Gaia: "I don't know – I'm not a seagull – but there must be other jobs you'd be good at.

"Wait a minute, can't you guys predict the weather?"

Sally: "We sure can. We can detect changes in air pressure that indicate when a storm is coming. That's when we fly inland to find shelter and to ride out the wind and rain."

Gaia: "That's pretty cool. Maybe you could do something with that."

Sally: "You mean like a weather girl? Or weather gull?"

Gaia: "Well…"

Sally: "Anyway, that doesn't solve my problem right here, right now."

Gaia: "I get that, but let's think about this."

Sally: "I don't need to think for long. If I had lots of money, it would solve all my problems."

Gaia: "Not necessarily. Having lots of money can be both a solution and a problem."

Sally: "Meaning?"

Gaia: "Meaning it can be a blessing and a curse.

"Look, I don't think there are any blessings in being poor – that's just not realistic – but I bet you can find some hidden blessings in a temporary financial setback, and I'm certain that's all this is."

Sally: "Have you had any such setbacks?"

Gaia: "Of course; everybody has. I've gone through periods when I've had very little money and I didn't know how I was going to pay my bills from one month to the next."

Sally: "So what did you do?"

Gaia: "Well, I very quickly learned the difference between need and want.

"I needed to eat, pay my debts, and keep fit and well so I could find work.

"I wanted to maintain my former lifestyle – eating at restaurants every week, my gym membership and holidays overseas – but those things weren't necessary, and something had to give, so I put them on hold for a while."

Sally: "That's where that phrase 'tighten your belt' comes in."

Gaia: "Exactly. Setbacks pass, but until they do, you have to make changes to adjust to your new situation. Those changes often reveal blessings in disguise.

"I turned my shopping trips into a game. Every time I went to the supermarket, I looked at different ways to save money. I searched for the special offers, bought generic brands only and used vouchers.

"I turned it into a competition with myself each week to see if I could save more than the week before."

Sally: "And did you?"

Gaia: "Yes, until I reached a point where I really couldn't do any better.

"I also rode my bike to work instead of driving my car, which meant not only did I save money on fuel but I also got fitter and lost some weight."

Sally: "Always a bonus."

Gaia: "Having no money toughened me up too. There's no gain without pain, they say.

"Struggling financially gave me more compassion and empathy. I'm not so quick to judge others now, because I know how easy it is to be doing great one minute, and then, like you, you only have to lose your job, and everything changes."

Sally: "I know what you mean. I have a strong desire to help others now too – such as all my friends who lost their jobs. I like to let them know where they can get a free meal."

Gaia: "Yes, but that shouldn't involve taking someone else's. People leave food behind, and you'll always find something in the bins or on the ground."

Sally: "Mmm..."

Gaia: "But you're right. When you come out of the other end, as you inevitably do, there's a strong compulsion to help others in the same situation.

"You have a shared experience – a common bond.

"Value and meaning become heightened in difficult times. The greatest celebrations come from the toughest battles."

Sally: "You should be a writer."

Gaia: "Now you mention it..."

Sally: "I know that, when I get back on track, I'll appreciate what I have more, after going through this turbulent time.

"I used to blow all my spare cash on going out and having fun, but I'll be more careful with it in future. I'll put some aside for a rainy day."

Gaia: "That attitude will serve you well in life."

"Good luck, and remember, *anche questo passerà* [this too will pass]."

Blessing bites

- Having lots of money won't necessarily solve all your problems.
- Money can be both a solution and a problem, a blessing and a curse.
- If you look hard enough, you'll find some hidden blessings in having to endure a temporary financial setback.
- Know the difference between need and want.
- You *need* to eat, pay your bills, pay your debts, and keep fit, well and healthy so you can work.
- *Wants* are nice, but they can be put on hold for a while when necessary. You can always come back to them when the storm has passed.
- Setbacks pass, but until they do, you have to make changes to adjust to your new situation. Those changes often reveal blessings in disguise.
- Try turning your situation into a game by looking for different ways to save money; this will help to ease any stress you might be feeling.
- Compete with yourself each week to see if you can save more than the week before.
- Having less money than you'd like can toughen you up and motivate you to find solutions.
- There's no gain without pain.

- When you're struggling financially, it can make you more compassionate and empathic towards others, as well as less quick to judge – and that can only be a good thing.
- When you come out the other end of a difficult financial situation, as you inevitably do, there's a strong compulsion to help others who are in the same situation you were once in.
- Shared experiences bond people.
- Value and meaning become heightened in difficult times. The greatest celebrations come from the toughest battles.
- When you get back on track after going through a turbulent time, you'll appreciate what you have even more.
- This too will pass.

Soul-family blessings

Ciao [hello]

Your soul family, or tribe, are people just like you. They think like you. They feel like you. They understand you, and you understand them – at a very deep level. You're bonded together through shared experiences, desires, goals, dreams, actions and suffering; and through energy and essence.

Your soul family doesn't judge you and won't desert you. They share the same mission and purpose as you.

They'll cradle you during your dark night of the soul. They're there to hold you when you crack open.

They're present to nurture, love, support, encourage and care for you as you transform and heal. They'll celebrate your achievements, successes, triumphs and victories as if they were their own.

They accompany you on the healing, sacred journey of your soul: your *Imramma*. Your soul tribe travels with you on the most important voyage of your life – that of discovering who you really are. You don't know where you're going, but your soul knows the way.

Your soul family knows that transformation and rebirth is painful. They're balm on your wounds. These people are a blessing.

Perhaps you've found your soul family, maybe you're still searching for your tribe or perhaps you need these people, but you don't know it yet.

They live all over the world. They're different sizes, shapes, colours, ages and faiths, and they've been here before. They have ancient wisdom, and they want to share what they've learned and know.

When you find your soul family, you know you're on your way home. The only thing you don't know is how long it'll take to get there. For some, there's no final destination when you travel with your tribe, but your journey feels safer. You feel cradled, and nobody judges you. Whether you're finding your way home or making the journey to see where it takes you, where you're heading is much more important than what you're leaving behind.

You'll live more authentically. You'll live your best life. You'll reach a higher level of yourself and greater self-awareness.

I found my soul family on Facebook. That's not surprising, really, given the prevalence of social media in our lives today.

Actually, I was guided to my tribe by a member who was a stranger, but she reached out to me when there was nothing left of me. She caught me, steered me towards the light, and then let me go when I was safe in the heart of my soul family. I'll always be grateful to her and thankful to the Universe for bringing her into my life when I needed her most.

My soul family is compassionate and empathic. They're selfless but careful to promote self-love, because you can't effectively help others unless your cup is full. You can't give if there isn't enough for yourself.

This family comprises healers, teachers, psychics, intuitives, carers, scientists, writers, athletes and homemakers. Where each works varies from in an office, outdoors or at home to in large corporations. They come from all walks of life.

They're warriors.

Your tribe could be anywhere: in your own home, next door, down the road, at work, on the internet or on the other side of the world – or spread across all of these.

You'll know when you meet your soul family. There's an unmistakeable knowing. You'll feel safe. You'll have hope. You'll feel protected. You'll dream big. You'll take inspired action.

You're the infant, and your tribe is like your nurturing mother. They'll break your heart with kindness.

Don't underestimate what your soul family can do for you and what you can do for them.

Find them. Cherish them. Respect them. Help nurture them the way they nurture you. You'll never look back. You'll be healed.

P.S.

Nigel Simpson

Perth | Western Australia

"I found my soul tribe or family when I was going through a difficult period in my life. My dad had passed away, and my mum and I together had to battle the bank in court for the property.

"I found a group of people who encouraged me to keep going and step out of my comfort zone. This gave me the confidence to keep going, and I decided that I was going to write my own script and how the story ends."

The blessing of rituals

Hello there!

Rituals are a blessing because they provide comfort. They're a hug when we need reassurance. They're a way to say thank you. They're a constant in a chaotic world.

The beauty of rituals is that you can create your own, copy someone else's, or follow rituals steeped in history or meaning. They're as bespoke as you are.

Morning rituals put you in a great frame of mind. They set the tone for how you want your day to unfold. It's up to you how you want your day to be.

It doesn't matter if things come at you from left and right, front and back, or above and below you. There will always be challenges, but how you perceive them and react to them does matter, because that will shape how you feel. So if you start your day feeling uplifted, the chances are that you'll continue to feel good, or at least not so bad, even when things sneak up on you and sideswipe you. It makes coping with life's niggles, frustrations and trauma a bit easier.

Most people already have a morning routine: shower and dress, drink coffee or tea, have breakfast, feed the cat and walk the dog. However, I'm talking about something more intrinsic to having a great day – something deeper.

You could light a candle; meditate; journal; pull an angel, oracle or tarot card for yourself for guidance; speak your gratitudes; sit in stillness; or listen to your intuition. Hold a crystal in the palm of your hand or to your heart, speak to it, and hear what comes back to you. Make beautiful patterns with them on a crystal grid. They're things of such beauty and a gift from Mother Earth – Gaia. Sing along to a song that makes you buzz. Walk in nature. Put your hands over your heart and whisper your desires to the Universe.

My suggestions are just some of the tools you can use to create rituals that feel right for you. Mix them up and make them your own.

There's no right or wrong with rituals. Whatever feels right for you is what's important, and you'll know what that is. For example, writing down on paper all the things you want to get rid of, whether they're habits, unwelcome thoughts, toxic people or worry – anything at all. Write down what you want to release from your life, and burn your list under a full moon.

Alternatively, you could think of 10 people or pets every day, and then silently bless them for the joy, love, meaning and support they bring, or have brought, into your life.

Blessing others is a selfless act, but it still makes us feel good. It's very gratifying to share our positive energy with someone else. For the time that you're focusing on another living thing, you're removed from your own troubles. So that's a double blessing! One for them and one for you.

All you have to do is wish them a blessed day. Bless them with good health, success, abundance, or whatever you think they want or need. It can be tailored to them or general. Here's an example:

> *I bless my beautiful dog, Daisy, today. I bless her with a happy walk in the woods, where she'll play with her friends. I bless her with good health, good food and a sound night's sleep tonight. I bless Daisy with love,* sempre e per sempre *[always and forever].*

There, that took only 15 seconds.

The world is full of rituals. Every country, culture and society has its own. Some are super elaborate, and some are very private and go unnoticed by all but those present. Nature has her rituals in every season.

Blessings come in the sense of purpose that rituals give us, the feeling of belonging to something, the feeling of being in control, doing something that makes us feel better, the comfort they bring and their permanence.

They change our mood, set our energy and make a sacred space to be.

You can take five minutes over your ritual or five hours, although I suggest the latter would be more of a luxury.

The hockey life wasn't what I wanted, but through it, I found the woman of my dreams

by Rick & Tammy Boyd

Houston | Texas | USA

On 25th December 1987, I was sitting in the kitchen of my parents' home in British Columbia, Canada, working up the courage to tell my father that I no longer had the desire to chase his dream of me playing professional hockey. As the beers flowed and my nerves calmed, I was about to break the news to him when the phone rang. The content of that call would change the course of my life forever.

I was invited to play for the Johnstown Chiefs semi-professional hockey team in Johnstown, Pennsylvania. With no time to think, it was decided that I'd give the game one more try. This was do or die.

I had no money to travel, so I asked the team to send me a plane ticket and some meal money to make it to the place where the iconic movie *Slap Shot* was filmed 10 years earlier with Paul Newman. Ironically, the movie is about a minor-league ice hockey team.

Once I was in Johnstown, and prior to playing a single game, a teammate and I were killing time by walking around the mall. We came across a ladies' clothing store in which a young woman was up a ladder creating a wall display.

We decided to go inside and look around. My teammate recognised a woman in the store whom he'd met previously, and it turned out that she was in the same sorority as the girl on the ladder, so we made small talk.

As the young woman on the ladder came down from her display and turned around, I was speechless. *Wow!* This was the cutest gal I'd ever set eyes on. I was done!

Although I thought she liked me, I later found out that she wasn't really impressed and thought I was a young high school hockey player who was interested in her as she was a college girl.

I was 23, and a college dropout. I was lost; I was trying to find my way and where I belonged.

Tammy was in her third year of college and working full-time at the clothing store, where she'd risen to become assistant manager. She didn't know that her world was about to be turned upside down.

After our first home game, which was a huge win, my teammate and I returned to our apartment rooms to change and get ready for a night out. As I sat in our kitchen, talking on the phone to my parents back in Canada, there was a knock at the door.

I went and opened it, and standing outside in a blizzard of snow flurries were 13 young ladies. The leader of the group asked if they'd found the party. To cut a long story short, I invited them in out of the cold and explained that they hadn't found the party, but we could certainly throw a party together, which is what we did.

The sorority sisters, who had set out from campus to find a party, ended up in my kitchen, and one of those ladies was that cute, shy girl from the ladies' clothing store.

We basically hit it off and started dating soon after.

The next several months were a mixture of the greatest moments of my life and the most heart-wrenching. I had no idea where I was going or how I was getting there. I was now involved with the most incredible person I'd ever met, and at times, I felt that I wasn't good enough for her. I made some bad decisions, which caused fights and heartache. I knew I needed to settle down, and I knew Tammy was the one, but I struggled with so many demons that, when things were going great, I'd do something stupid and self-destructive, which would ruin the best thing that had ever happened to me.

Now let's not forget that this perfect woman had a strong mind, high expectations for herself and the people around her, and she was now seeing the world's worst procrastinator. I was also a heavy-drinking, irresponsible idiot.

I stayed in Johnstown and played out the remainder of the hockey season, and then I stayed with Tammy and her parents.

Our dating life had its ups and downs, break-ups, and make-ups, but those are for another book or story. We'd reached a point where we'd decided to end things after another stupid move on my part.

I left Johnstown in the summer of 1988.

In the fall of that same year, I attended my first national-hockey-league training camp and was assigned to a minor-league team in Indiana. With a couple of weeks to go before the start of the season, I returned to Johnstown and spent some time with Tammy. Only this time, I was even worse than previously. We ended up having a major falling out and ending our relationship. Once again, this was no fault of hers. It was all on me.

I left Johnstown again and reported to Indianapolis to start the 1988/89 season, but I knew something was missing. I was missing the only woman who had ever put me in my place, and who had taught me more about having a good work ethic and determination than anyone else. Not having her by my side left a major void in my life.

Later that fall, we had several long conversations about our relationship and what would have to happen to work things out. I made every effort, she visited Indiana, and I knew that I wanted to spend the rest of my life with her.

At Christmas 1988, I travelled back to Johnstown to spend a very short Christmas break with Tammy and her family. In my bag, I'd brought along an engagement ring that I planned to give to Tammy when I asked her to be my wife.

Thank goodness she said yes when I asked.

We celebrated by attending a Christmas Eve church service with her family, followed by a Christmas party with friends. We then had a short night together before I had to return to Indy.

Tammy continued her senior year of university whilst I lived and worked more than 500 miles away. It wasn't the best situation for a newly engaged couple, but we made it through.

As the season wound down and we were making plans for a summer wedding, Tammy called me to break the news that we were about to become parents. Wait, *what?*

Not everyone was happy that a baby was on the way. I was excited and couldn't wait, but Tammy was still in school and spent the latter part of her senior year dealing with the pregnancy and managing a clothing store, whilst her future husband played hockey and lived in another state.

At the end of the hockey season, I returned to Johnstown and picked up whatever work I could, including landscaping and car sales. But there wasn't much employment, and I didn't have a green card, so we decided to spend the summer back in Canada, where I could work and Tammy could focus on keeping herself healthy for the baby.

It turns out this wasn't the best plan, as Tammy – who had always been on the go – was now stuck out at the farmhouse my parents rented, with no direct contact with civilisation. My gorgeous, young wife was now living her worst life, with no family, no job and a growing belly, whilst she was in a place that was known for its beaches and summer fun in bikinis, and with a husband who was never there.

We made it through the summer and made our way back across the country in our small Nissan Sentra, with everything we owned packed in the car. We were back in Pennsylvania with Tammy's parents, but I had to leave for training camp, and once again, she was alone.

Halfway through the six-week training camp, I got a call to say that Tammy was going into labour. I flew home and was with her for the last part of her 27-hour-plus labour. It was determined that our sweet baby girl had a rather large head, meaning there was little chance she was coming out on her own, so a successful caesarean section was completed. We were now a family of three.

However, I had to return to Hartford, leaving behind a brand-new mother with our baby girl. The hockey life was never the life I wanted or dreamed of – it just sort of happened – but through it, I found the woman of my dreams.

A month or so later, I was assigned to play in a minor pro-league in Indiana, but I decided to return to Johnstown to be with my wife and baby instead.

After I'd returned, we moved into a small apartment complex, and Tammy started her planned career as a schoolteacher. However, in early January, I was offered the chance to play hockey in a higher league that paid more money. Without hesitation, I agreed, but when I broke the good news to my young wife, I soon realised that I'd forgotten the most important thing: we were now a family, a team, and decisions such as this needed to be discussed and agreed upon together. This wasn't what Tammy wanted for us, and it was a rough couple of nights prior to me leaving. Once again, this young mother was by herself with a new baby.

I chased the hockey career for the next few years, playing in several states and leagues, but never climbing to the top. It wasn't meant to be for a guy who needed to be pushed to work out and eat properly, and, well, I just honestly didn't put in the work required to play at the highest levels. That's the truth.

Our family dynamic was built on the back of a very strong, independent woman who had caught my eye the first week I was in a new town. She'd led the way in showing me, and then our children, how to secure success and a good life.

Some of the highlights and lowlights over the next few years included Tammy taking our girls, Tiffany and Calsie, to their track meets, and they both competed in beauty pageants with great success. At the same time, the girls were on high school cheer and travel squads that competed nationally.

It was the travel squad's success at the national level that drew the attention of the ABC TV network. ABC had a long-running program called *Wife Swap*, where two families switch lives for two weeks and try to change or understand how other people live. The *Wife Swap* production team contacted our gym, where the girls did cheer, and asked them to recommend a competitive family. Our name was given to the network, and we were eventually invited to participate on the show.

The experience was eye-opening for everyone in ways we could never have predicted. As we were heading down a path of not knowing where we'd be as a married couple after the kids moved on to college, it was very interesting to get a taste of life without my wife. I was lost.

The new lady in my life, who was sent to us from the network, was a very sweet woman who babied her husband and son to the point where it was almost odd. She did everything for both of them, and the son just played video games with his very immature father, who quite possibly didn't have a job.

But this woman did bring out the fact that, as a family, we spent way too much time running around the place trying to make games, competitions and pageants, and we never stopped to take time for us.

This had been another blessing in disguise for our family. First, a hockey career that I was ambivalent about but which led me to my beautiful wife and, ultimately, my children. Now, a stranger was highlighting the cracks in our lifestyle that could be harmful to our family. As the saying goes, there's a reason for everything.

As a postscript, our son, Cody, has played hockey all over the USA and Canada. To play junior hockey one year, he even returned to Johnstown – the town he grew up in and where his father started his hockey career. He also went on to win a championship in my home province of British Columbia in Canada.

So, hockey brought us together, drove a wedge between Tammy and I at times, earned me a living once, and provided a career for our son.

In the meantime, Tammy and I worked hard to find time for ourselves and to rekindle a relationship that had been through so much. We had some long conversations and spent a lot of time reflecting on the challenges, the ups and downs, the kids, the early years, the journey we'd been on together, and how most people would never have stuck together through the things we endured.

I was never the easiest person to get along with. I wasn't easy to tame and was never one to take orders. We got married young and whilst Tammy was pregnant. We never had a chance to dance and travel as a young couple, but neither of us would change that for anything now.

Today, we live in Texas and have built a better life here. We live each day smiling as the sun comes out and the temperature rises. When the door opens and our granddaughter, Emery, comes walking in, it brightens up the entire house.

As we look back, and as I write this, I can say it has been emotional. The road wasn't always paved with gold, but that didn't stop us. We met on a cold night in 1988, and we came from two very different worlds, but we managed to create a successful, loving, hard-working family.

Spiritual awakening

Yhi: "Why do bad things keep happening to me?"

Gaia: "What bad things?"

Yhi: "How long have you got?"

Gaia: "As long as you need."

Yhi: "I barely know where to start."

Gaia: "Sometimes, bad things happen to flag up changes you need to make to your life so you can be true to yourself. If you keep ignoring the red flags, bad things keep happening."

Yhi: "So you're saying it's my fault?"

Gaia: "I don't know what's happened to you, but I'm saying you might need to ask yourself if you're responsible for at least some of the bad things you say keep happening to you.

"We ignore red flags when we're too attached to a particular outcome or person. We don't want to consider a different scenario or being without that person.

"But when we're able to put our fears and our need to control everything to one side, we loosen our grip, and life is so much more peaceful. It's less stressful."

"So, when you say bad things keep happening to you, it's likely because you keep ignoring the signs to take action and change some aspect of your life."

Yhi: "How do you get to that point? Where you're so comfortable in your own skin that you don't care what happens."

Gaia: "It's not about not caring. It's the opposite, actually. It's caring about you, rather than caring too much about an outcome or being too attached to another person."

Yhi: "I think I'm following what you're saying. I've got a friend who went through a really difficult time, and he's come out the other end a completely different person. He's calmer and more confident. He says he's had a spiritual awakening."

Gaia: "Good for him. Adversity often leads you to being more spiritually aware or enlightened, and that's definitely a blessing."

Yhi: "What does 'spiritual awakening' even mean?"

Gaia: "Personally, I think it can mean different things to different people, but for me, it means my heart, mind, body and soul are all in sync.

"And when that happens, my life is blissful."

Yhi: "My friend has been transformed for the better. Nothing much phases him any more. He can still get upset, worried or angry – like the rest of us – but it doesn't last long. He seems to be able to solve any problems that come up, because he's got a different way of looking at things."

Gaia: "It sounds like he's at peace with himself. Spirituality gives you that and so much more: confidence, trust and knowing that all will be well. It's a very safe place to be."

Yhi: "It's like he's woken up from a long sleep, and he's the same person, but different, if that makes sense?"

Gaia: "Yes, it does."

Yhi: "Anyway, you said a spiritual awakening is a blessing. Why is that?"

Gaia: "Because it gives you more insight and awareness. It's like all your senses have been magnified. It's like putting on some special glasses, and then all the colours are much more vivid.

"When you have that, you have a greater understanding of what's good for you and what's bad for you. You make better choices. You're less likely to trip yourself up or let anyone else do so, for that matter.

"When you understand yourself and how you work, you can change your life for the better."

Yhi: "How long does that take?"

Gaia: "It never ends. You'll always be a work in progress. It's like saying, "When will I have learned everything there is to know?" The answer is never, because you're always learning.

"I think a spiritual awakening is also a bit like the ugly duckling story. You have to go through the ugly to get to the beautiful, but the journey is so worthwhile and the destination – if there is one – is even better."

Yhi: "So if I wanted a spiritual awakening, where would I start?"

Gaia: "With wanting one, basically, and that will probably be because you've hit rock bottom and have nowhere else to go.

"Then, you'd read books about it, listen to podcasts on YouTube, learn to meditate and speak to like-minded people. One thing leads to another to another to another.

"Just follow the path that opens up to you. It's like going on a road trip without a map. It's very exciting."

Yhi: "It sounds like hard work."

Gaia: "It's not; it's great fun. It can become addictive because you start to feel better straight away.

"Hard work is when your heart, mind, body and soul are all out of alignment. Then, you're not living your best life. You're often living it for someone else, and that sucks."

Yhi: "I get that last bit. I feel like everyone else is pulling my strings."

Gaia: "Amongst other things, a spiritual awakening encourages you to surrender to what is, to go with the flow and to trust in something bigger than yourself.

"It's scary at first, but let me give you an analogy that'll help you understand."

Yhi: "If I surrender to what is, people will walk all over me and use me as a doormat."

Gaia: "Not if you know what you want and take action to get it. You have to get to that place first.

"I'm going to use the river analogy because everyone knows and understands it. It's tried and tested.

"If you find yourself upstream in the river, you have two choices. You can go with the flow and allow the water to take you around the boulders, past the sandbars and away from the whirlpools, and let it deposit you where you're meant to be.

"Or you can fight the flow. You can grasp at a boulder, and then what?

"You leap onto a sandbar, and then what? You'll have to get back in the water to continue your journey. You're just delaying the inevitable.

"You can swim against the flow to reach the shore, only to find that there's nothing there for you. It's barren, and you're exhausted."

Yhi: "OK, I get that, but how will I know if I've had a spiritual awakening?"

Gaia: "You'll just know. You'll be more intuitive. You'll listen to your gut and be guided by what it tells you.

"You'll lose your attachment to people and things, because you're enough. You'll feel calm and confident.

"You'll develop healthy boundaries. You won't be held hostage by other people or circumstances.

"You'll see, hear and smell signs too, and you'll know it's not a coincidence, because they happen too often, and they're in sync with what you want, think and feel."

"When I started writing this book, the words 'blessing', 'blessings in disguise' and 'silver lining' kept popping up. I saw them everywhere: in books, on the TV, on my phone and on social media. Other people spoke the words. They aren't words or phrases that you'd expect to see and hear all the time, but I did, so I knew I was on the right path. I felt guided.

"Before that, when I started waking up to who I truly am, I kept seeing repetitive numbers. It still happens – all day, every day. It's a part of my life now."

Yhi: "What do you mean?"

Gaia: "Every time I look at my phone, Facebook, my computer, the microwave clock or even a vehicle number plate – it doesn't matter what it is – I see repeating numbers such as 10:01, 555, 13:31, 2222 and 18:18."

Yhi: "What do they mean?"

Gaia: "I look them up to find the messages behind them. I believe that they're there to guide me, and that they relate somehow to the energy or vibration I'm giving off at that moment.

"Some people believe that the Universe, angels and spirit guides use numbers to communicate with us. At the end of the day, it's up to you how you want to interpret them and whether you want to use them as a tool to help yourself."

Yhi: "That sounds a bit woo-woo. How do they help you?"

Gaia: "Because different repetitive numbers have different messages of guidance, encouragement and support. I can apply them to the way I'm feeling or thinking, or to something that's happened. It's a bit like talking to a friend for advice. So one sequence might suggest that I need to take more time for myself; another will guide me to make a decision about something. It's up to me what I do with that information."

Yhi: "Something similar happened to me.

"My favourite archangel is Ariel because she's the angel of nature, and I love nature. The image of the lion is associated with Ariel. I spoke out loud to Ariel and asked for help when I was upset about something, much like someone prays to God.

"Do you know what? I kept seeing lion pictures everywhere. I'd turn on the TV, and there would be a lion with her cubs. I clicked on my foreign language app on my phone, and the word ‘lion’ jumped out at me. I picked up a book, and there was another you-know-what. I could give you so many examples, but it went on and on.”

Gaia: “You were getting signs, and it’s up to you how you want to interpret them and what you want to do about them, if anything. I’d say that, when your energy changes and your heart, mind, body and soul are in sync, the energy creates signs for you to act upon.

“It’s not rocket science. It’s just about being more in touch with yourself.”

Yhi: “It’s a shame you have to go through hell first before a spiritual awakening comes knocking at your door.”

Gaia: “They can be spontaneous, but yes, it does seem to be the case that spiritual awakenings are triggered by life-changing events or trauma.”

Yhi: “But then, as you say, the blessing is that you live your life on your terms, more authentically, and that’s got to be a good thing.”

Gaia: “*E l’unico modo di vivere.* [It’s the only way to live.]”

The blessings in nature

Hiya ♡

There are blessings in nature and in the seasons, and many of them mirror the cycles in our own lives.

Spring | Primavera

Spring is the season of new beginnings – rebirth.

We're blessed with fresh buds. The first bulbs of the season push through the soil and bloom. Fresh, new leaves appear on trees. Animals awaken and come out of hibernation. The temperature in the northern hemisphere gets warmer. The ground thaws. The earth comes to life slowly after her long sleep. The landscape morphs from monochrome into vibrant colour.

There are many blessings in a new beginning. It's a chance to start again. You get to wipe the slate clean. You can take stock of what should stay and what can go because it no longer serves you. It's an opportunity to do things differently and get them right this time.

This is our time to grow into the person we came here to be, to wake up to our full potential, to be big rather than small, and to be loud rather than silent.

Spring is full of hope and the promise of a brighter tomorrow. It's a mood-changer. It's transformation at its exquisite best.

Summer | Estate

This is the season when everything flourishes, because summer shares her light, warmth and energy. Plants and trees bear fruit. The warmth encourages animals to breed. The days are long, and the nights are short. The insects are abundant and busy; you'll hear them before you see them.

Nature is bountiful.

This beautiful bounty triggers something inside us: an aliveness, and a need to live in the moment, to have fun, to enjoy and to soak up the beauty all around us.

It instils a desire to be carefree. This is why we came here. This is why we transformed.

It helps us to know that what we have now is enough. There's no attachment, because we've loosened our grip. There's no looking back and no looking forward; there's only the here and now.

Autumn | Autunno

The leaves change to a vivid colour before they flutter to the ground. These are fire shades of yellow, orange, red and brown. The grand display of colour is nature's standing ovation before the final curtain draws across this season.

Branches are left bare. The temperature changes. Plants throw their seeds to the ground so animals can collect them and start preparing for the cold months ahead. Plants stop making food. Everything in nature begins to shut down – in slow motion.

Autumn is a time for harvest, for gathering and for storing.

Birds fly to warmer climates. Some animals migrate.

Nature begins to conserve her energy and draw down her eyelids.

As our energy is drawn inwards, this is also a time to clear out the clutter in our mind and to consolidate existing rituals or create new ones. This is the season of planning and preparation.

It's a time to embrace change, because there's nothing more rewarding than reaping the harvest we sowed in the form of the goals and intentions we set at the start of the year. This is our celebration.

Winter | Inverno

Winter is stark, but there's magic in the air. The ice, frost and snow have a light all of their own. Empty birds' nests are revealed in the trees and hedges.

Many plants need shorter days and low temperatures to become dormant. This way, they store up energy for new growth.

Winter tests us and tests our resolve. This is where we learn to deal with challenging people and situations. This is where the work is done so we can emerge fully formed into spring.

We have to be still, to conserve our energy, to bed down, and to keep warm and safe. The cold forces us to go within ourselves and to rest. We're given this season to quiet our souls. The stillness allows us to create a space to listen, feel and be.

This self-care allows each of us to fill our tank, and when our tank is full, we can better serve others.

The results of this season mean that, when we awaken in the spring, the cycle of life and blessings can continue.

Primavera

by Alan Brett

Primavera means 'coming first'.
It means the coming of spring.
The first of seasonal cycles,
Which nature's blessings bring.

Past is the winter of discontent,
With better times to come,
As nature wakes the sleepers,
Those who sing and others dumb.

First emerge the snowdrops
In Vestal Virgin white,
Their heads all bowed in modesty;
A truly wondrous sight.

To seduce the early insects,
From early morn to night,
To ensure they'll come again
When another spring brings light.

Crocuses too, so colourful,
Vie for insects' favours,
With flowers on the fruit trees
For later seasons' flavours.

And among the leaves and refuse,
Littered all around,
Emerges the gilded primrose,
With flowers that abound.

Whilst daffs blow golden trumpets
To herald St David's Day,
"*Dydd Dewi Sant,*" they say in Wales,
As they nod their heads in play.

The sight and smell of flowers
Isn't all there is to spring,
We see, nesting in their bowers,
Birds wooing as they sing.

Each season brings its blessing,
And each can bring its woes,
But spring is rather special,
As everybody knows.

When your dreams come true

Hello again...

Having a dream is such a blessing. We all need something to hold on to, to aspire to and to work towards.

Dreams can be wispy, fleeting, or distractingly enduring and intense.

A dream is an adventure waiting to happen, a goal to focus our energy and attention on, a distraction from mundane chores, or a carousel ride with a final destination – one you created.

A dream's gift is that it's yours to fill up with whatever and whoever you like. It's the sweet shop of the mind.

When your dream comes true, the blessing is so much greater and your positive feelings are massively magnified. A wish fulfilled is a beautiful and very precious thing.

The seed of my dream was planted long, long ago, but I turned to it and nurtured it during a spectacularly chaotic time in my private life, which coincided with the Covid-19 pandemic.

Holding my dream in my heart, mind, body and soul was an escape from a life I hated. I took inspired action to make my dream happen, because you have to do the work and play your part. And ultimately, *eccolo* (there it is)! It came to magnificent fruition almost a year later.

My dream manifested into my reality when I needed it to most.

I'd always wanted to visit the extraordinary Galapagos Islands in the Pacific Ocean and to swim with sharks. That's exactly what I did, but more than that: I swam with sealions, turtles, iguanas, penguins, octopuses, stingrays, diving cormorants and jelly fish too.

I met the most amazing like-minded people, some of whom will be my lifelong friends.

I walked around many of the unique islands that make up the volcanic archipelago. I woke in the early hours of every morning, when the sky was still *nero* (black) and the stars were so bright; it was as if the Universe had super-charged her fairy lights. One star was bigger and brighter than all the others. According to my new friends, it was the planet Venus.

Every day began with a different showpiece view. The sound of water slapping against the yacht was ever-present, as was the remarkably tame wildlife.

I was blissed out, overjoyed, at peace, content and living authentically. I wanted for nothing. My cup was full. I was intoxicated on being in the present moment.

So why am I telling you this?

My dream came true as a blessed consequence of a bad situation. I might have – and probably would have – got around to booking this holiday of a lifetime at some stage, but pain and discomfort pushed me forwards. They're exceptional triggers for positive action.

Was my chaotic life a blessing? I didn't think so at the time, but I know it was now.

Ask yourself these questions:

* What dreams do you have?
* When were they planted?
* What can you do to nurture them?
* What's happening in your life that can give your dreams momentum?
* What inspired action can you take to bring your dreams into reality?
* Are you prepared to play your part to bring them to fruition?

Dreams don't just happen. You have to work at manifesting them, but if you do, the Universe will meet you halfway.

That sounds like a pretty good deal to me!

Alba returns

Gaia: "Hey there, Alba. Is that you?"

Alba: "Yes, it is. Hi."

Gaia: "How are you? I've been thinking about you since we last met."

Alba: "I've lost my mum."

Gaia: "I'm so sorry. My heart goes out to you and your family."

Alba: "Thank you. It was unexpected, so it was a terrible shock. I know she was ill, but her death was still sudden."

Gaia: "That's awful; you had no time to say goodbye."

Alba: "No, there wasn't, and that will always haunt me. I was getting ready to go to see her when she passed away. I don't know why she didn't wait for me."

Gaia: "Perhaps she was protecting you. She didn't want you to see her passing."

Alba: "I've been thinking about the things we talked about when I last saw you, and I can honestly say there are no blessings in my mum's death."

Gaia: "Of course not; that goes without saying. The blessings are in the lifetime of memories that you created together and now have of your mum. No one can take them from you or change them. They're yours for keeps."

Alba: "Yes, I know, but they're of little comfort at the moment."

Gaia: "That's because it's all still so raw, but they'll be a comfort to you in time.

"There are stories that will be passed down through the generations of your family. The gifts you gave each other will be a constant reminder that she's never far from you. You've probably kept cards and letters that she wrote to you. There are photos of her. There will be all sorts of things that keep her close, even though she's not visible any more."

Alba: "I did spend more time with her than I would have otherwise, after you and I spoke, and I bought her things to make her life more comfortable. I took my laptop into the care home and played one of her favourite ballets to her. I said the things that needed to be said.

"I feel my family and I did everything we could for Mum under the circumstances. We couldn't have done more."

Gaia: "I'm sure that's the case."

Alba: "I like to think that Mum will return to nature somehow. Maybe she'll come back as a flower or a butterfly? Something nice and pretty.

"In fact, we scattered her ashes beneath a beautiful rhododendron I bought my dad, so every time it flowers, it'll remind us of Mum."

Gaia: "I think that's a lovely way to look at things. I believe people leave an energetic footprint, so your mum has just changed shape or form or colour."

Alba: "You said that we sometimes need to use our imaginations to feel better, so I've been doing that; I've been playing mind movies to feel at peace."

Gaia: "Does it help?"

Alba: "Sometimes. A bit. It depends on how I'm feeling on the day, but the more I practise, the more it becomes a habit."

Gaia: "That's better than 'no.'"

Alba: "I also like to think of Mum as travelling ahead of us, rather than leaving us behind. It feels less final, and it gives a sense that we'll see her again one day."

Gaia: "Do you believe that?"

Alba: "I'm not sure what I believe, but I know what I'd like to believe, if that makes sense?"

Gaia: "It does. People with faith – and faith can be anything you want it to be – seem to cope better when bad things happen. Faith gives hope, and we all need a bit of hope."

Alba: "If Mum's just travelling ahead, we'll all catch up with her one day and be together again."

Gaia: "It's a lovely thought."

Alba: "It's a comforting thought."

Gaia: "Another thing I like to think is that your mum is only a breath away. Think about that. Really think about what that means. Just one breath away. How close is that?"

Alba: "Wow. I like that. Anyway, Mum's at peace now – no more suffering – and I like to think that she's catching up with all her family and friends who have gone before her."

Gaia: "Maybe they're all sitting around a big table, eating and talking."

Alba: "Arguing, more like."

Gaia: "Ha! Like that, was it?"

Alba: "They were fiery Italians, so yes, it was like that."

Gaia: "That memory just made you smile."

Alba: "So it did. Another thing that makes me smile is that the dreadful stress my father suffered when he was caring for Mum at home reignited his passion for poetry. Writing helps him cope, and it's very cathartic.

"More than that, he actually publishes his poems in his local community magazine, and he enters writing competitions. He belongs to a creative writing group, where he's made new friends, and some of his poems have even found their way into this book."

Gaia: "You're going to be OK. There will be triggers now and again, but they'll become less frequent and less severe over time."

Alba: "I know I'll be OK, and one of the biggest blessings at the moment is that I have wonderfully supportive family and friends."

Gaia: "I don't know how people cope without them at a time like this."

Alba: "Neither do I, but one thing I know for sure: I'll never take them for granted. Despite what's happened, I count my blessings every day for the people I still have in my life."

Gaia: "That's lovely and a beautiful way to see things."

Alba: "Now, I'll focus on my father. I'll support him as best I can and make sure we spend as much quality time together as possible. Every day counts."

Gaia: "And just go with the flow. Don't force anything. Life is easier when you surrender to what is and let the Universe pick up the slack. It's more peaceful. You play your role, and let the Universe play it's part."

Alba: "Like characters in a play."

Gaia: "*Il gioco della vita.* [The play of life.]"

Alba: "Where the end is simply another beginning – chapter one of a new narrative."

Gaia: "Exactly. Every ending signals *nuovo inizio* [a new start]."

Alba: "*Ogni nuovo inizio è una benedizione.* [Every new beginning is a blessing.]"

Blessing bites

- Sometimes, a person who's dying doesn't wait for their family to gather around their bedside to say a final farewell, because they want to protect them.
- When someone we loves dies, the blessings lie in the cherished memories created together. They're your comfort blanket. No one can take them from you or change them. They are yours forever.
- Your memories should comfort you in time. Maybe not in the early days, because your feelings are still so raw, but in time, you should be able to smile, rather than cry, when you think of your lost loved one.
- You can keep someone's memory alive in so many ways. You could pass stories down through the generations of their family. The gifts you exchanged are constant reminders, as are cards, letters and photos. Planting a tree, bush or shrub in their memory or scattering seeds is a lovely way to create a living reminder. You are limited only by your imagination.
- You need to do whatever feels right for you to keep someone close to you after they die.
- As long as someone remembers you, you never really die.

- There's some small comfort in knowing that you did everything you could for the person who passed away, so as to make their life as safe, comfortable and meaningful as possible.
- If you believe that people leave an energetic footprint, you can imagine your loved one returning as something beautiful in nature. Sometimes, we have to use our imaginations to feel better and to feel at peace.
- It may help to imagine that your loved one is travelling ahead of you, rather than leaving you behind. It feels less final and gives a sense that, one day, you'll be reunited.
- People with faith – and faith can be anything you want it to be – seem to cope better when bad things happen. Faith gives hope.
- Your loved one is only a breath away, and that's really close.
- There will be things that trigger your sadness now and again, but they'll become less frequent and less severe over time.
- There's a saying that time heals all wounds. For some, that may well be true, but for others, time is more likely to make your feelings softer and gentler – a bit easier to live with.

Bless this book

My final hello!

May this book be blessed and all who read her.

I bless the heartfelt words and sentences within these pages, and the time you've spent to take them in and make of them what you will.

They're designed to comfort, inspire and motivate you; to cradle you when you feel too broken or tired to go on; and to give you hope when you feel strong enough to put one foot in front of the other.

There's enough love and energy in the tens of thousands of words in this book to lift you up, so I hope you rise in your power, just like I did.

I give thanks that my words flow from me to you. It's such a blessing.

I bless the many people who have contributed to this beautiful, divinely inspired book. Thank you for sharing your thoughts and feelings; memories and stories; and artistic, written, spoken and technical skills. I bless that you gave these things willingly, and with love in your heart, so that others may benefit.

I bless happiness, because finding it and holding on to it are what this book is all about. We each have within us a strong and enduring desire to be happy, yet it seems to be such a difficult thing to achieve. The reasons for that could fill a book, but that's for another time and place. When we have happiness, we want to keep it because we know how wonderful it makes us feel. When we don't have it, we seek it, and we suffer when it feels out of reach.

I bless the sources that made the paper for this book. I bless the technology that allows me to upload my book online so people around the world can buy it. I bless the fact that you'll like this book (I hope!) enough to recommend it to your family and friends.

If the words and stories in this book help one person, then it has done its job.

I bless creative energy, and so much of that has gone into this book. It truly is a blessing. I started with a single blank page and have finished with chapters full of beautiful words that breathe their own unique blessings.

I hope these words captivate your imagination such that you'll be able to live the life you deserve – the life we all deserve.

Words are a blessing, and beautiful words are divine. Beautiful words wrap around you like a soft, warm, safe blanket. They say, "Come here, and I'll look after you."

Words keep us all connected. They impart our thoughts and feelings, and our wants and wishes. They take us on a journey. They change colour, shape and texture. They paint pictures. They lift our hearts. They open us up and expose us to new opportunities.

The right words at the right time can ameliorate our soul.

A sentence is a necklace of words. What a magical and blessed image!

Look closely at the letters in each word you write, and you'll see how every word speaks its own unique language through the shape, curl, line and flourish of each letter as it moves towards its full-stop destination.

Words are fluid. They move back and forth, in and out, and over and under. They move through you and around you.

Dolce (sweet) words sprinkle your soul with sweetness.

Funny words make you laugh, and laughing is so good for the soul. It's so transformative.

Happy words feel like sunshine, and who doesn't like sunshine?

Words are forever. Once written or spoken, they can never be taken back, so choose your words carefully. Make sure they come with love, respect, kindness and compassion. Bless them before they leave your lips or pen.

Make your words beautiful, and see what comes right back at you.

There's boundless energy and meaning in words. I could whisper, "I love you," so softly that you couldn't be sure if breath had escaped my lips, or I could scream, "*I love you!*" from the top of a mountain. Both whisper and scream would be impactful, but in different ways for each person who is gifted them.

'Blessing' is a beautiful word. It's full of gratitude, and gratitude is love. It sounds like an adventure, a promise and a distraction from the mundane.

In the right hands, words can do all sorts of amazing things. They can do so much good. They can praise, support, encourage, nurture, cradle, stroke or mend a broken heart in an instant.

So I bless each and every word in this book, and in so doing, I pass the blessing on to you.

Sii benedetto. (Be blessed.)

365 Blessings

I hope you've enjoyed reading about blessings in general and blessings in disguise. I hope too that the real-life stories have inspired you to look for those gems when things are going well in your life, as well as when they're not.

If nothing else, they can take the edge off a difficult day or situation. They can change your perspective and lift you up.

Sometimes, as you've read, hidden blessings can be life-changing and life-enhancing. They're magical because you don't always see them, but they are there. They often enter your life when you most need them, need to change direction, need transformation or need a guiding hand.

Blessings can ebb and flow, like the tide on the seafront where Gaia has her conversations. They can blow around like tumbleweed. They can come out of nowhere, like a bolt of lightning, or they can be slow burners. Sometimes, you can feel them manifesting, and you know that something better is on its way to you.

Now it's your turn to reflect on your own blessings by finding them in your every day. Occasionally, they'll jump out at you, and there'll be so many you won't know which to choose. At other times, you'll have to work hard and dig deep to find a blessing because it'll be in disguise.

But all I can say is give it a go. It's better to try and fail than fail to try.

Now it's over to you to identify a blessing every day of every month for one year. When the chips are down, you can look back on your blessings over a 12-month period and, literally, count how lucky you are.

These should give you hope that things can change and get better. They can be your ladder to help you climb out of the abyss.

So, grab your notebook and a pencil (then if you want to make changes, you can just rub out what you've done and start again), and write down the hidden, or not so hidden, blessings that have lifted your heart.

Keep this easy and get into the habit; your entries can be as simple as this:

APRIL

1st A motorist let me pull out when I was running late for work.

2nd I got some money off my shopping today.

3rd A stranger smiled at me, which made my day!

4th

5th

6th

Contact Me with Your Stories

I really hope you've enjoyed the stories in this book, particularly the real life ones that came from my family and friends. It was so generous of them to share their blessings in disguise, and they were expressed in such a heartfelt way. I believe they add something authentic to the pages of this book, and I trust that they helped someone somewhere to feel more inspired, empowered and motivated, and less alone.

I hope the stories have brought comfort to those who were seeking it.

Every person is unique and so is every person's story. When we share our personal experiences, it's not only an act of selflessness but it also helps to support others who may need a helping hand, guidance or direction.

I'm now looking to collect stories from my wonderful readers to include in a follow-up book. I would love to hear from you if you're happy to share your stories about blessings that looked and felt more like a curse at the time, but turned out to be something wonderful – and for the best.

Has something happened to you that you didn't like, want or expect, only for it to turn out to be the best thing that ever happened?

Did you set your heart on renting or buying a particular house, but miss out on getting it, only to end up with something much better later on?

Did you miss your plane, boat or train only to find out that it was just as well, for whatever reason?

There are hundreds and thousands of stories out there, waiting to be told, and they will give hope to people who are facing challenges and obstacles. They could just be the lifeline that someone is looking for.

If you'd like to contribute to a future volume, I'd love to hear from you.

Please contact me on lisa.brett0604@outlook.com or via my website, www.LisaBrettAuthor.com.

Thank you so much in advance. I really look forward to hearing from you, and until I do, I wish you and your loved ones many blessings.

Namaste.

About the Author

Lisa's dearest wish is to help others to help themselves, in order for them to find happiness again when life throws them a mega curve ball – or several.

By empowering people to improve their lives, you give them freedom and quality of life. She believes that everything you need to change things for the better already exists inside you.

Lisa was born in Sydney, Australia, but she currently lives in England. She has dual nationality and has spent her life living and working in both countries.

She began her writing career as a TV reporter and newsreader before 'going to the other side' and working in politics as a media advisor to cabinet ministers.

A desire to work from home, so she could spend more time with her beloved dog, Daisy, saw her ultimately establish a successful business as a family celebrant.

Lisa has always loved reading self-help and personal growth books, which she was introduced to by a friend during a metaphorical bump in the road. *Learned Optimism* by Martin Seligman put her in the driving seat to help herself when life suddenly pushed her into the wrong lane.

Since then, she has also had a spiritual awakening. This happened during the darkest period of her life, and it has culminated in writing *Finding Happiness When It Hurts*, which she felt divinely guided to write.

Acknowledgements

My deepest love and gratitude goes to my beloved family, friends and spiritual soul family around the world, who supported me in writing this book. Many of them also contributed to it with their unique stories.

These same people loved, nurtured and encouraged me during the traumatic period in my life that ultimately spawned this book. Their presence then and now is valued more than they know.

In particular, I thank my wonderful father, Alan, as I inherited my writing ability from him. He also contributed a compelling story and two poems, and he has acted as editorial assistant on this book.

I thank my beloved late mother, Piera, who – as an Italian – provided the inspiration for using the most beautiful of languages to spice up the pages in my book. Sadly, she never knew that I've become an author, but she'd have been so proud of me.

I thank my beautiful sister, Jane, for being the best sister in the whole wide world. She's my best friend, supporter and confidante.

I thank my brilliant brother-in-law, Salvador, for being the best thing that ever happened to our family.

I thank Samantha Faulkner for her beautiful, delightful and

enchanting illustrations. They give extra meaning to my words and help bring the pages to vibrant life. The butterflies are particularly special. They're deeply meaningful because of the massive transformation they each undergo.

I'm profoundly grateful to my beloved dog, Daisy Boo, for giving my life meaning and purpose at a time when it would have been easier to exit this world. She quite literally saved my life.

I thank all the staff at The Book Refinery for their support, guidance, expertise and professionalism at every stage of publishing my book. Their collective talents have vividly brought my book to life so readers around the world can feel comforted, inspired and motivated to find the hidden blessings in adversity.

Contributors

Alan Brett

Anita Lenzo

Salvador Jimenez

Jane Brett de Jimenez

Amparo Gabela

Dr Pamela Schulz OAM

Erick Jimenez

Teresa Misser

Zerah Garrote

Cilla Peck

Carmen Jimenez

Amanda Lynch

Nigel Simpson

Rick & Tammy Boyd

What's Next?

I'm creating a 'comfort notebook' with beautifully crafted messages between the pages where you can make your notes. It'll be a notebook you'll want to keep, long after you've filled all the blank pages, because the unique messages will comfort, inspire, guide and motivate you to strive for a happier, more authentic, life. There'll be a beautiful message for every week of the year, so not your average notebook.

A follow up book to this one is also planned that will focus on the real life stories of you, my readers. My market research tells me that one of the things you want to read more about is how others have overcome adversity. These precious stories will give others hope and help people to feel less alone.

When we read about how others have dealt with the same or similar issues, we are instantly united in a common bond which can feel very reassuring.

In addition, I aim to translate this book into other languages, starting with Italian and Spanish.

You can keep up to date with my follow up book and the comfort notebook via my website: www.LisaBrettAuthor.com and sign up to my email newsletter for all the details.